The Guide To
Houseplants

The Guide To
Houseplants

Illustrated by Tamara Dubin Brown

Produced by
The Philip Lief Group, Inc.

GRAMERCY BOOKS
New York

This 2001 edition is published by Gramercy Books™, an imprint of Random House Value Publishing, Inc., 280 Park Avenue, New York, NY 10017, by arrangement with The Philip Lief Group, Inc.

Gramercy Books™ and design are trademarks of Random House Value Publishing, Inc.

Illustrated by Tamara Dubin Brown
Produced by The Philip Lief Group, Inc.

Printed in the United States of American

Random House
New York • Toronto • London • Sydney • Auckland
http://www.randomhouse.com

Library of Congress Cataloging-in-Publication Data

Guide to houseplants / illustrated by Tamara Dubin Brown.
p. cm.
Rev. ed. of: The houseplant encyclopedia / Maggie Stuckey. 1993.
"Produced by the Philip Lief Group, Inc.".
ISBN 0-517-16281-4
I. House plants—Encyclopedias. I. Brown, Tamara Dubin. II. Stuckey, Maggie.
Houseplant encyclopedia.

SB419 .S785 2001
635.9'65—dc21   00-050394

9 8 7 6 5 4 3 2

Contents

The Guide To
Houseplants

1

❧ ❧ ❧

The Joy of Houseplanting

What is it about green plants that makes us want to grow them inside our homes?

For those of us who love being in the outdoors, it's a way to bring a little piece of the outdoors inside. For those of us who live in cities, in concrete towers, far away from a country road and anything green, it's a way to connect, in some small way, with a lifestyle we sometimes wish for. For those who enjoy watching something grow, it's a way to participate in the process. For whatever reasons our hearts hold, having plants inside is a way to bring the world of nature up close, where we can enjoy it at our own pace.

There are more mundane reasons too. Houseplants are wonderful ways to decorate rooms when you don't have a lot of furniture. They serve as movable room dividers. They substitute for curtains or blinds, screening out unpleasant views while providing their own green curtain. They add sparkle to our rooms with a splash of color or perhaps a sweet aroma. They provide a healthy sense of satisfaction, give us something to brag about, and perk up our spirits. All this for a small investment in time and just a few dollars. Not bad.

Houseplants Through the Ages

Human beings have been growing plants inside their domiciles for centuries. As far back as ancient Roman and Greek civilizations, people grew plants indoors in containers. But things really began to take off with the age of exploration, as Europeans began to visit other parts of the world and bring back the treasures they found there. These explorers went to the Far East in search of spices and silks, and later to the New World in search of gold and whatever other forms of wealth and adventure were to be had.

On these expeditions, the adventurers were joined by serious botanists and other scientists, who found in the new lands species of plants that were new to them. With great excitement, they collected samples of these new species and brought them back home, where other scientists studied, analyzed, and named them.

It turned out that plants from the more tropical areas of the world would live indoors, in hothouses and greenhouses. This was a charming novelty to Europeans, whose knowledge of plants was limited to the species that grew around their homes, outdoor plants that needed a certain temperature range and would surely keel over inside.

Exotic plants became something of a fad for the wealthy. The royal houses of Europe sponsored botanical expeditions, sending their personal gardeners to Australia, Japan, the South Pacific, and North America to collect new specimens. Aristocratic families competed with each other for elaborate gardens and greenhouses; one sign of status was the number of rare plants in the family greenhouse.

Finding the plants in the remote areas of the world was dangerous; getting them home safely was something of a gamble. Ship captains considered plants a nuisance and resented giving up good drinking water to keep them alive. Then a London doctor named Ward accidentally discovered that plants could live in glass containers with very little water, and Wardian cases came to be used to transport the specimens on the long voyage back to Europe.

Back home, the horticultural industry felt the effect of this strong interest in exotic plants. Nurserymen too sent plant collectors to the far ends of the world in search of new plants, but their main contribution was their research work at home. As the new plants produced seeds, the nurserymen began to experiment with the seedlings, searching for the growing conditions that would produce the strongest plants. Before long they were crossbreeding, producing hybrids from two different species. Then for the first time it was possible to visit a commercial greenhouse, purchase a plant that had been imported from another country or propagated from such a plant, and grow it indoors in a container.

The houseplant industry had begun.

Throughout the nineteenth century, only the wealthy could afford houseplants. Then, as nurseries gradually developed mass production methods, as transportation systems became more efficient, and as merchandising techniques became more sophisticated, that began to change. Indoor plants were soon within the reach of the middle class, and by the middle of the twentieth century you could buy a small philodendron plant in almost any Woolworth's anywhere in the country, at real dime-store prices.

The houseplant boom had begun.

Today, indoor plants are available throughout the country in all kinds of locations. There are large greenhouses and nurseries, small specialty shops that sell just houseplants, florists, and garden centers. Many large variety stores have garden sections, and so do supermarkets, corner markets, and five-and-dime stores (if you can find one).

The plants you find in today's stores have behind them years of breeding and experimenting for sturdiness and disease resistance. And today there are literally thousands of new varieties that did not exist a hundred years ago. Horticulturists are constantly developing new strains, new colors, new varieties for us to enjoy. Almost every day, new ones appear in the shops. Those adventurous souls who sailed to the New World so long ago and brought back the plants they found there, would be amazed.

It's Easier Than You Think

Perhaps you have the impression that growing houseplants is tricky, or takes a kind of mysterious wisdom that only some people are blessed with. If so, you can relax: the plants are tougher than you think. All those nursery people have worked all these years to develop strains that are hardy indoors, and growing them successfully is not difficult. In many, many cases, the plants practically take care of themselves. To illustrate, I'd like to tell you a personal story.

In 1989 my sister gave me a pretty basket filled with several small plants: a prayer plant, a dieffenbachia, a croton, and two peperomias. She had removed the plants from their original two-inch pots, along with the soil, and put each one in a "sock" made from old panty hose (she's very creative, my sister). She arranged the plants in their socks artfully in the basket, filled in the spaces with sphagnum moss, and tied a pretty Christmas bow on top.

The socks were intended to be temporary; her idea was that after enjoying the basket through the Christmas season, I would take each plant out and transplant it to its own pot, where it could grow at a normal pace. And I fully intended to do that. But, life being what it is, I never quite got around to it.

Now, more than four years later, they are all still in the basket. By all the rules they should have died by now, or at the very least stopped growing. Instead, each one has grown vigorously, with hardly any attention from me except watering and a little fertilizer in the summer. Today the basket is filled to overflowing with rich, gorgeous foliage in a wonderful range of colors; everything is bursting with health. Book logic tells me I should move the plants out into individual pots, but I'm not going to do it. Those plants have settled into an environment in which they are thriving, individually and collectively. And I'm not going to touch it.

Common Sense and Philodendrons

Having healthy houseplants doesn't take black magic, green thumbs, or anything else mysterious. All it takes is common sense.

The most important thing is to get the right plants to begin with; don't handicap yourself. Learn the basics about light, water, and humidity, and stick to plants that need what you can give them. You probably won't make major changes in your house to accommodate the plants, so buy plants that need what you already have. If you don't have lots of windows, for instance, buy only plants that will live in low light.

Also, choose plants that match both your life and your personality. If you're out of town frequently, buy only plants that don't need lots of watering. Stay away from plants that are the opposite of your natural style: if you know you just want to enjoy the plants without a lot of work, don't choose the kind that need constant attention.

There's a reason philodendrons are the most popular houseplants in the world—they're about the toughest plants you can buy. So if you're getting started, choose one of the plants that are easy to grow. If you buy a plant that's wrong for your personality or wrong for your house, you're asking for trouble.

Commonsense Rule #1

It's easier to be successful when you buy the right plant in the first place.

1. Buy plants whose needs match the conditions in your house. Be realistic.

2. Buy plants whose needs match your personality and your lifestyle. Be honest.

3. Buy plants that are easy to take care of, not hard. Be sensible.

Chapter 2 is all about making the right choices. At the beginning of the chapter you'll find a checklist that will help you sort out the significant ingredients in your life and your home that have an effect on your houseplant purchases.

The trick to keeping a houseplant healthy is to duplicate, as much as reasonably possible, the growing conditions of the plant's natural home, the place in the world where the plant grows wild.

Sometimes we forget that houseplants are really domesticated outdoor plants. Just as city kids can't picture milk in any container except a plastic jug, we tend to think of houseplants exclusively as something that grows in small plastic pots at the greenhouse. But your houseplant didn't originate in the plant store. You bought it there, and they bought it from a nursery, and they grew it from a seed or a small cutting, but way back in the beginning, somewhere in the world—the jungles of Brazil, the South African desert, a tropical rain forest—the plant was growing wild. The small plant you just bought at the plant store has the same genes as its forebears, and it needs the same general growing conditions.

The philodendron that sits tamely in your living room window is a native of South American jungles, where it grows into a monstrous vine with leaves big enough to hide under. If you want it to thrive, you'll try to give it the environment its genes are used to: warm temperatures, high humidity, rich, moist soil, and bright indirect light. A cactus is a desert plant; it craves lots of bright sun, loose sandy soil, and not much water.

All this boils down to a very commonsense way of taking care of your favorite plants: as much as realistically possible, try to give them the conditions they would have if they were growing wild in their natural home.

Commonsense Rule #2
In your house, as much as possible, give your plant the same conditions it would have in its natural environment.

To explain this, let me tell you another personal story. I recently bought a small maidenhair fern (*Adiantum*). It's a beautiful plant but not the easiest thing to grow.

Varieties of the delicate *Adiantum* are found all over the world, principally in the humid climates of semitropical rain forests. A few species grow in North America. In the Pacific Northwest, where I live, one breathtakingly beautiful variety grows in the wet forests of the Cascade Mountains, in the shadow of the Douglas firs and big-leaf maples. The ferns die back in the winter and slowly begin to unfurl their delicate foliage in the early summer.

So this is how I remember what they need as houseplants: I picture them growing along the hiking trail that runs by the stream, where it is cool at night and warm with muted sunshine during the day, where the soil is damp and the atmosphere is always moist.

Unless you live in Florida or Hawaii, you won't see many houseplant species growing wild, in their natural conditions. But if you take a minute to picture the native environment of the species commonly grown as indoor plants, you will develop an instinctive sense of what they need. You won't have to stop and research each plant; just think of them in general categories. Pretty soon you'll be saying to yourself: "That's a jungle plant," or "desert conditions," or "cool rain forest," and you'll know what to do.

So, adding this all together, we arrive at one all-purpose rule: buy the plants that are appropriate for your house and your lifestyle, and then give them the care that mimics their native environments. And then relax and enjoy their beauty.

After that, there is one other point that must be made: Sometimes you can do all the right things and the plant dies anyway. Maybe it had some disease when you bought it but wasn't yet showing any evidence of trouble. Maybe you set it outside for a breath of fresh air in the summer, and it got sick. Maybe it was grown in a poor environment before you acquired it. Maybe your neighbor overwatered it while you were on vacation.

Or maybe it was destiny. Quite a few species that look wonderful in the plant store simply will not live forever in your house; you should think of them as temporary.

Whatever the case, keep your perspective. This was a plant, not a person or the family pet. Unless you bought a piece of living sculpture, you probably paid somewhere between $5 and $15 for it. That's about the same as you would pay for a pretty bunch of cut flowers, and you *expect* them to be temporary.

So if your $10 plant gave you pleasure for a year and then decided to kick the bucket, that's still a pretty good deal. If you liked that particular species, go out and get another one, and have the fun of watching it grow all over again.

Commonsense Rule #3
Sometimes houseplants die. It isn't the end of the world.

What About Those Latin Names?

No doubt you have noticed that houseplants have two kinds of names: something unpronounceable in Latin, and the "normal" name by which sensible people call it. The Latin name is its scientific name, and the other is its common name. Why two?

Because plants are friendly, and sort of like family, over the years people gave them a friendly name. The problem is, people in different parts of the world, even different parts of the country, don't all use the same common name.

If your new neighbor asked you about "mother-in-law's tongue," would you realize she was talking about the tall, skinny succulent you call "snake plant"? That one plant has two common names. It works the other way, too: the same common name can be applied to two very different plants. Have you ever seen a "watermelon plant"? Was it a *Pilea cadierei* or a *Peperomia argyreia*?

That's why scientific names are important. Every plant has one, and only one, scientific name. If a research botanist from Japan, a nursery worker from England, a garden club member from New Orleans, and a houseplant enthusiast from Phoenix all happened to be in the same room talking about *Hoya carnosa* 'Variegata', they would know with certainty which plant they meant—and they would all mean the same one. Latin is used because it's the closest thing we have to a universal language.

Because common names are not the same in all parts of the country, plants in this book are listed according to their scientific name. At the start of the encyclopedia (chapter 3), there is a cross-index of common names. And the index at the back of the book lists all plants by both common names and scientific names.

If working with the Latin names is new to you, let's take a minute to get acquainted. It's not as difficult as you think.

Genus and Species

First, the entire plant kingdom is divided into categories and subsequent subcategories:

> Division
> Class
> Order
> Family
> Genus
> Species

We're concerned with only the last two—genus and species. All plants that share certain botanic similarities belong to the same genus; each genus can have several species. (And sometimes there are subspecies and varieties, but we'll get to that in a minute.) Often plants are grouped into a genus because of certain cellular characteristics that are not apparent to the naked eye, so members of a genus may not necessarily resemble each other—some do, some don't.

Let's look at one name: *Philodendron oxycardium*

> *Philodendron* = the genus name
> *oxycardium* = the species name

The genus name always comes first, the species second. It's somewhat like people's names:

> McNamara, John
> McNamara, Mary

One difference is that with plants you would never say just "oxycardium." The species name is not used by itself.

So *oxycardium* is a certain kind of philodendron; there may be (and in fact there are) other kinds. If we were talking about the entire philodendron genus, and mentioned several species, we could abbreviate all names after the first, like this:

> *Philodendron oxycardium*
> *P. selloum*
> *P. radiatum*

Notice, too, that in this case the scientific name has become the common name: a philodendron is a philodendron.

Commercial growers and botanists are constantly at work developing new items for us to enjoy. These are not totally new species, just new varieties of existing species. (The correct term for these greenhouse-developed varieties is "cultivar," which means **cult**ivated **var**iety.) When you see a third word in a Latin name, it's a subspecies or variety. *Dracaena marginata* 'Tricolor' is a variety of *Dracaena marginata:*

> *Dracaena* = the genus
> *marginata* = the species
> 'Tricolor' = the variety

Pronunciation and Meaning

If you ever studied Latin in school, you remember that its vowel sounds are conveniently consistent. There's none of the confusing business that English has: "through," "bough," "rough," and "dough" have the same vowel spelling but very different pronunciations. With Latin, once you learn a vowel pronunciation in one word, it will be the same in others.

Besides, you already know how to pronounce quite a few Latin names:

philodendron	chrysanthemum
begonia	asparagus
citrus	schefflera
narcissus	rhododendron
gardenia	

In chapter 3, you'll learn how to pronounce the scientific names. Each Latin name is spelled phonetically, using the closest equivalent English word or sound. For example:

Dracaena = drah-SEE-nah

The capital letters indicate the syllable that gets the emphasis in pronunciation. That is really the only tricky part of dealing with Latin words: putting the emphasis in the right place. And if it's wrong, it sounds very wrong indeed.

Here's an example. There is a group of attractive outdoor shrubs that have small leaves, red or orange berries, and a low, spreading way of growing that's very handsome in rock gardens. The genus name is *Cotoneaster*. If you just read that word, and never heard anyone pronounce it, you might very well say "cotton easter." But it is actually pronounced "coh-tone-ee-ASS-ter."

One small disclaimer is needed. Over the years, the botanical names of many familiar garden plants have been Americanized in their pronunciation. The way they are pronounced by most of us who enjoy plants or work in the gardening field is not exactly the "pure" Latin pronunciation you might encounter on a college campus or in a botany text. You and I and David, that smart young man who works in the local garden center, would call a weeping fig a "fye-cuss"; the Latin professor would call it a "fee-cuss." But since we're far more likely to be conferring with David about our weeping fig than with the Latin professor, we'll call it a "fye-cuss," and that is the pronunciation given in this book.

What do the words mean? Sometimes they describe a characteristic of the plant. For instance,

recurvata means "curved"
floribunda means "many flowers"
macrophylla means "big leaf"
pendula means "hanging down"

(Just for the fun of it, what do you think *Nautilocalyx forgetii* means?)

Sometimes they indicate the plant's original home: *japonica* means Japanese; *australis* means from Australia. Sometimes they honor a person, often the botanist who worked with a certain species: *hoya* or *benjamina* or *hahnii*. And sometimes they don't mean anything in particular; the names were just chosen. After all, what does ''McNamara'' mean?

Using This Book

Keeping in mind the overall commonsense guideline—choose the plants that match your house, not the other way around—a good way to get started with plants is to review the questionnaires in chapter 2. These will help you evaluate any limiting conditions in your life that you should keep in mind as you decide which plants to buy. Then study the lists in chapter 2 for categories that match your particular situation; those are the plants you will find easiest.

In the encyclopedia section (chapter 3), you will find individual descriptions, including illustrations, of the plants, along with detailed directions on how to take care of them. They are listed alphabetically, by scientific name; a cross-list of common names is found at the beginning of the chapter.

The next four chapters show you how to take care of your plants, using the same commonsense approach.

Chapter 4   Explains the things you need to do to your plants on a regular basis—watering, fertilizing, and so on.

Chapter 5   Tells you how to interpret your plant's distress signals, and what to do about them.

Chapter 6   Explains, in step-by-step detail, how to repot a plant, something you do only occasionally. That's the time you need to know about different kinds of pots and potting soil.

Chapter 7   Shows you how to make baby plants from the parents you have on hand—a very satisfying process.

Chapter 8 demonstrates how to plan and plant terrariums and dish gardens, two popular and easy ways to show off your favorite plants. Chapter 9 provides answers to the houseplant questions that come up most often—miscellaneous items not covered in the earlier chapters, or perhaps key points restated in a different way.

2

🍒 🍒 🍒

Houseplants for Every Home: Choosing the Best Ones for You

Success with houseplants is largely a matter of choosing the right ones in the first place. If you fall in love with a temperamental beauty that looks fine in the greenhouse but will pout in a normal living room, you're just asking for trouble.

You need to think honestly about your life, your schedule, and your personality: how much time and effort are you able—or willing—to devote to taking care of plants? And you need to take a look around your house, evaluating it from the plants' point of view. The reality is, you aren't going to completely change the environment inside your house to suit the plants; the trick is to choose plants that match the home environment you already have.

Choosing plants involves a balance between aesthetics and practicality. Certainly you want plants that look attractive to you; you also will be smart to choose those that will be easiest for you to manage, considering your house and your lifestyle.

Ask yourself these questions:

Evaluate Your House

√ What room do you plan to put the plant in?
√ How cold is that room at night in winter?
√ How hot is that room in summer?

✓ Does every part of that room get the same amount of light, or is one side dimmer than others?

✓ Do you know what compass direction the windows in that room face?

✓ Is there usually a draft in some part of that room?

✓ Is there lots of human traffic in the room where the plant will be?

Now look at the particular space you have in mind.

✓ How big is it? Do you know how big the plant eventually gets?

✓ How close is it to light? Do you know how much the plant needs?

Evaluate Your Decor

✓ What is the overall decoration style of the room? For instance, is it formal, casual, modern, antique, Scandinavian, Oriental?

✓ Do you have a decorating theme in the room, such as English hunt, Southwestern, country? If so, does the plant enhance that theme, or fight it?

✓ What is the predominant color scheme?

✓ Do you know if the plant blooms, and if so what color?

✓ Is there an architectural element in the room you want to disguise? (You can do that with a large plant.)

✓ Is there something in the room you want to highlight, such as an interesting architectural feature, a special piece of furniture, a piece of artwork? (You can do that with a plant strategically positioned nearby.)

✓ Is there furniture, carpet, or flooring that might be damaged if water were spilled on it?

✓ Considering the overall look and feel of the room, what "visual texture" should the plant have:

    tall and spiky

    tall and wide

    big and dramatic

    small and eye-catching

soft and fluffy
draping, trailing

Evaluate Yourself

What kind of parent to a houseplant do you have the time (or inclination) to be?

√ Are you out of town often? For long periods of time?
√ Are you forgetful by nature?
√ Are you a procrastinator?
√ Do you have a complicated daily routine, with little extra time and frequent crises?
√ When you have hobbies, do you usually spend lots of time with them? In the past have you maintained interest in hobbies for a long time, or do you tend to lose interest quickly?
√ Do you like to tinker? Do you enjoy becoming actively involved, in a hands-on way, in things you're interested in?
√ Are you intrigued with the idea of making little plants from the ones you now have?
√ Will other people in your household be helping take care of the plants? Are they careful, or casual?

If you think about these questions honestly, you should have a sense of how "plant dedicated" you can realistically be. And you should have a clear picture of the growing environment in the rooms in your house. With those two pictures in place, look through the lists in this chapter; which categories describe you and your house?

Plants Grouped by Growth Characteristics

Small Plants

At full size, these will be less than one foot tall or long.

Adiantum　　　　　　　　*Dracaena godseffiana*
Asplenium nidus　　　　　*Echeveria elegans*
Cactus (most species)　　*Fittonia*

Iresine	*Saintpaulia*
Kalanchoes	*Sansevieria trifasciata* 'Hahnii'
Peperomias	Succulents
Pileas	*Tolmiea menziesii*

Medium Plants

When full size, these will be between one and three feet tall.

Aglaonema	*Maranta*
Asparagus 'Sprengeri'	*Nephrolepis exaltata*
Aspidistra	'Bostoniensis'
Aucuba japonica	*Pandanus veitchii*
Bromeliads	*Plectranthus australis,*
Ceropegia woodii	*P. oertendahlii*
Chlorophytum	*Polypodium aureum*
Cissus antarctica,	*Pteris ferns*
C. rhombifolia	*Sansevieria trifasciata*
Cyrtomium falcatum	'Laurentii'
Davallia	*Sedum morganianum*
Dracaena deremensis	*Setcreasea purpurea*
Epipremnum aureum	*Spathiphyllum*
Gynura aurantiaca	*Syngonium*
Hedera helix	*Tradescantia*
Hoya carnosa	*Zebrina*

Large Plants

Under good conditions, these plants will reach more than three feet tall (or long).

Araucaria excelsa	*Crassula argentea*
Beaucarnea recurvata	*Cycas revoluta*
Chamaedorea elegans	*Dieffenbachia*
Chrysalidocarpus lutescens	*Dizygotheca elegantissima*

Dracaena fragrans,
  D. marginata
Fatshedera lizei
Fatsia japonica
Ficus benjamina,
  F. elastica,
  F. lyrata
Grevillea robusta
Howea forsteriana

Monstera deliciosa
Philodendron hastatum,
  P. oxycardium,
  P. selloum
Podocarpus gracilior
Polyscias fruticosa
Rhapis excelsa
Schefflera
Schlumbergera

Ten Super-Easy Plants

Aglaonema
Aspidistra
Chlorophytum
Dieffenbachia
Dracaenas

Monstera
Philodendron oxycardium
Plectranthus australis
Sansevieria
Spathiphyllum

——————— ———————

Green Thumb Tip

Looking for very tough plants but not sure which ones to choose? Check your favorite shopping mall.

The plants in those nice planter boxes that decorate indoor malls and the lobbies of office buildings are chosen for their durability. People bump into them, spill coffee on them, blow cigarette smoke on them—and they still live. They get little or no sunlight, extremes of air-conditioning, and who knows how much watering—and they still live.

So figure out which plants they have in the mall (take this book along if you need to), and buy the same ones for your home.

Plants That Are Easy to Grow

Aglaonema
Araucaria excelsa
Asparagus 'Sprengeri'
Aspidistra
Asplenium nidus
Aucuba japonica
Beaucarnea recurvata
Cactus
Ceropegia woodii
Chlorophytum
Cissus antarctica,
   C. rhombifolia
Crassula argentea
Dieffenbachia
Dracaena (any)
Echeveria elegans

Epipremnum aureum
Ficus (any)
Howea forsteriana
Hoya carnosa
Monstera deliciosa
Pandanus veitchii
Peperomias
Philodendrons
Plectranthus australis
Sansevieria
Sedums
Spathiphyllum
Syngonium
Tradescantia
Zebrina

Plants for Offices

Subject to variations in temperature, and irregular waterings by different people, plants for offices need to be very tough.

Aglaonema
Aspidistra
Cacti
Cissus antarctica,
   C. rhombifolia
Dieffenbachia
Dracaenas
Fatshedera lizei
Ficuses
Howea forsteriana
Monstera deliciosa

Palms
Pandanus veitchii
Philodendrons
Podocarpus gracilior
Sansevieria
Schefflera
Succulents
Syngonium
Tradescantia
Zebrina

Plants for Low-Light Areas

Few plants actually prefer dim light, although many will
adjust to it. Therefore this list includes plants that are also
found on the moderate-light list.

Adiantum
Aglaonema
Asparagus 'Sprengeri'
Aspidistra
Asplenium nidus
Beaucarnea recurvata
Ceropegia woodii
Chamaedorea elegans
Chlorophytum
Chrysalidocarpus lutescens
Cyrtomium falcatum
Davallia
Dieffenbachia
Dracaenas
Epipremnum aureum
Ficus lyrata
Hedera helix

Howea forsteriana
Monstera deliciosa
Nephrolepis exaltata
  'Bostoniensis'
Pandanus veitchii
Philodendrons
Pileas
Plectranthus australis
Podocarpus gracilior
Pteris ferns
Sansevieria
Setcreasea purpurea
Spathiphyllum
Syngonium
Tolmiea menziesii
Tradescantia
Zebrina

Plants for Moderate Light

Adiantum
Aglaonema
Araucaria excelsa
Asparagus 'Sprengeri'
Aspidistra
Asplenium nidus
Beaucarnea recurvata
Ceropegia woodii
Chamaedorea elegans
Chlorophytum
Chrysalidocarpus lutescens

Cissus antarctica,
  C. rhombifolia
Cycas revoluta
Cyrtomium falcatum
Davallia
Dieffenbachia
Dizygotheca elegantissima
Dracaenas
Epipremnum aureum
Fatshedera lizei
Fatsia japonica

Ficuses
Fittonia
Grevillea robusta
Gynura aurantiaca
Hedera helix
Howea forsteriana
Hoya carnosa
Kalanchoe tomentosa
Maranta
Monstera deliciosa
Nephrolepis exaltata
  'Bostoniensis'
Peperomias
Philodendrons

Pileas
Plectranthus australis
Polypodium aureum
Polyscias fruticosa
Pteris ferns
Saintpaulia
Sansevieria
Schefflera
Sedum morganianum
Spathiphyllum
Syngonium
Tolmiea menziesii
Tradescantia
Zebrina

Plants for Bright-Light Areas

Few houseplants (other than cacti and succulents) can take a steady diet of direct sunlight. Most of the plants on this list prefer what is usually called "bright indirect light," meaning that it is reflected off a wall or mirror, or "bright filtered light," meaning that a sheer curtain blocks out the direct rays of the sun. This list includes plants that either need bright light for survival, or will tolerate it without damage.

Asparagus 'Sprengeri'
Beaucarnea recurvata
Cacti
Ceropegia woodii
Chlorophytum
Cissus antarctica,
  C. rhombifolia
Codiaeum variegatum
Crassula argentea
Echeveria elegans
Fatshedera lizei
Fatsia japonica
Ficuses

Gynura aurantiaca
Hedera helix
Howea forsteriana
Kalanchoe blossfeldiana
Plectranthus australis
Podocarpus gracilior
Polypodium aureum
Sansevieria
Schefflera
Schlumbergera
Sedum morganianum
Setcreasea purpurea
Succulents

Plants That Need High Humidity

Adiantum
Asplenium nidus
Cyrtomium falcatum
Davallia
Dizygotheca elegantissima
Fittonia
Grevillea robusta
Gynura aurantiaca
Marantas

Nephrolepis exaltata
Pandanus veitchii
Pileas
Polypodium aureum
Polyscias fruticosa
Pteris ferns
Saintpaulia
Schefflera

Plants That Need (or Will Tolerate) Low Humidity

Aglaonema
Beaucarnea recurvata
Ceropegia woodii
Chlorophytum
Chrysalidocarpus lutescens
Crassula argentea
Dracaenas
Echeveria elegans
Fatshedera lizei

Ficuses
Hedera helix
Plectranthus australis
Podocarpus gracilior
Sansevieria
Sedums
Setcreasea purpurea
Tradescantia
Zebrina

Plants for Cool Rooms

Adiantum
Araucaria excelsa
Aspidistra
Aucuba japonica
Beaucarnea recurvata
Fatshedera lizei

Hedera helix
Plectranthus australis
Pteris ferns
Tolmiea menziesii
Zebrina

Plants for Warm Rooms

Aglaonema
Asparagus 'Sprengeri'
Aspidistra
Beaucarnea recurvata
Cacti
Ceropegia woodii
Chlorophytum
Chrysalidocarpus lutescens
Codiaeum variegatum
Crassula argentea
Cycas revoluta
Dieffenbachia
Dizygotheca elegantissima
Dracaenas
Echeveria elegans
Epipremnum aureum
Fatshedera lizei
Fatsia japonica
Ficuses

Fittonia
Gynura aurantiaca
Howea forsteriana
Hoya carnosa
Kalanchoes
Maranta
Peperomias
Pileas
Plectranthus australis
Podocarpus gracilior
Rhapis excelsa
Saintpaulia
Sansevieria
Schefflera
Schlumbergera
Sedum morganianum
Setcreasea purpurea
Succulents
Syngonium

Plants for Hanging Baskets

Adiantum
Asparagus 'Sprengeri'
Ceropegia woodii
Chlorophytum
Cissus antarctica,
   C. rhombifolia
Davallia
Epipremnum aureum
Ficus pumila
Fittonia
Gynura aurantiaca

Hedera helix
Hoya carnosa
Nephrolepis exaltata
   'Bostoniensis'
Philodendron oxycardium
Plectranthus australis
Schlumbergera
Sedum morganianum
Syngonium
Tradescantia
Zebrina

Plants That Climb

Climbing plants thrive when fastened to any kind of support: a pole or moss stick in the pot or a trellis around the window.

Cissus antarctica,
    C. rhombifolia
Fatshedera lizei
Hedera helix
Hoya carnosa

Monstera deliciosa
Philodendron bipennifolium,
    P. hastatum,
    P. oxycardium
Syngonium

Plants That Grow in Water

If you root cuttings of these plants in water, and don't get around to putting them into pots promptly, you don't have to worry—they can live in water for months on end.

Aglaonema
Dieffenbachia
Dracaena
Epipremnum aureum
Fatshedera lizei
Hedera helix

Philodendrons
Plectranthus australis
Schefflera
Syngonium
Tradescantia
Zebrina

Plants That Don't Need Frequent Repotting

In this list are plants that for one reason or another don't need to be repotted every year; some because they actually grow better when they are tight in the pot, others because they grow slowly. Most of these can go two, three, even more years in the same pot.

Aglaonema
Aspidistra
Beaucarnea recurvata
Bromeliads
Cacti

Chamaedorea elegans
Chlorophytum
Crassula argentea
Cycas revoluta
Dracaenas

Echeveria elegans
Fatshedera lizei
Ficuses
Howea forsteriana
Hoya carnosa
Maranta
Podocarpus gracilior

Polyscias fruticosa
Rhapis excelsa
Sansevieria
Schlumbergera
Sedum morganianum
Succulents

Big Plants for Drama

Araucaria excelsa
Aucuba japonica
Beaucarnea recurvata
Chrysalidocarpus lutescens
Cycas revoluta
Dieffenbachia
Dizygotheca elegantissima
Dracaena fragrans,
   D. marginata
Fatsia japonica

Ficus benjamina,
   F. elastica,
   F. lyrata
Grevillea robusta
Howea forsteriana
Monstera deliciosa
Philodendron bipinnatifidum,
   P. selloum
Poaocarpus gracilior
Rhapis excelsa
Schefflera

Plants That Flower

Plants on this list will produce some flowers indoors, although some are small and not significant. The most spectacular flowers are on bromeliads, saintpaulia, and schlumbergera; it is for their flowers that we grow these plants.

Bromeliads
Cacti (most, eventually)
Ceropegia woodii
Chlorophytum
Hoya carnosa

Kalanchoe blossfeldiana
Maranta
Saintpaulia
Schlumbergera
Spathiphyllum

Plants with Colorful Leaves

These plants have leaves with bright colors—either a solid color (rare) or a color mixed in with green (more common); leaves with mixed colors are called "variegated."

Aglaonema
Aucuba japonica
Codiaeum variegatum
Dieffenbachia
Dracaena godseffiana,
  D. marginata,
  D. m. 'Tricolor',
  D. fragrans
  'Massangeana'
Epipremnum aureum

Fittonia
Gynura aurantiaca
Hoya carnosa 'Variegata'
Iresine
Maranta
Plectranthus oertendahlii
Setcreasea purpurea
Tradescantia
Zebrina

Plants with Unusual Leaves

The leaves on these plants are all green (not colored or variegated), but interesting for their texture, shape, or general appearance.

Beaucarnea recurvata
Kalanchoe daigremontiana,
  K. tomentosa
Monstera deliciosa
Peperomia argyreia,

P. caperata 'Emerald
  Ripple'
Philodendron selloum
Pilea 'Moon Valley'
Sedum morganianum

3

🍒 🍒 🍒

The Plant
Encyclopedia

In this section, you will find descriptions and how-to-grow information for most of our common houseplants. They are organized alphabetically, by scientific name. To help you find the plants you're interested in, there is also an extensive cross-index of common names.

One comment about organization: Many species that we enjoy as houseplants belong to the same genus; there are, for instance, a number of philodendrons available in the plant store. Because genus name appears first in scientific nomenclature, and because the plants here are listed alphabetically by scientific name, you will find all the philodendrons together.

If different species of the same genus look quite different from each other, or are equally important as houseplants, each one is described and illustrated separately. If they are similar in appearance and have similar requirements, just one species is described in detail and the others are mentioned only briefly.

Each plant description includes a phonetic spelling of the Latin name, so that you can learn the pronunciation. Sometimes these "how they sound" spellings use actual English words (such as "penny" and "stair"); sometimes they are phonetic renderings of the individual sounds of each syllable, following these guidelines:

This sound	As in the word	Is spelled
long "a"	pay	ay
short "a"	cap	a
short "a"	fall	ah
hard "c"	cup	c
soft "c"	cinder	s
long "e"	me	ee
short "e"	bet	e
long "i"	lie	ye (or eye)
short "i"	pin	i
long "o"	so	oh
short "o"	top	o
long "u"	you	ew
short "u"	too	oo
short "u"	full	u

And remember that the syllable that should be emphasized is printed in capital letters, like this:

fill-oh-DEN-drun (for Philodendron)

Common Name	Scientific Name
African evergreen	*Syngonium podophyllum*
African tree grape	*Cissus antarctica*
African violet	*Saintpaulia*
Airplane plant	*Chlorophytum*
Aluminum plant	*Pilea cadierei*
Areca palm	*Chrysalidocarpus lutescens*
Arrowhead vine	*Syngonium podophyllum*
Artillery plant	*Pilea microphylla*
Asparagus fern	*Asparagus densiflorus* 'Sprengeri'
Asparagus fern	*Asparagus setaceus*
Baby rubber plant	*Peperomia obtusifolia*
Balfour aralia	*Polyscias balfouriana*
Ball cactus	*Notocactus* (see Cactus)
Ball fern	*Davallia*
Bamboo palm	*Rhapis excelsa*

Common Name	Scientific Name
Barrel cactus	*Echinocactus* (see Cactus)
Bear's paw fern	*Polypodium aureum*
Beefsteak plant	*Iresine herbstii*
Bird's nest fern	*Asplenium nidus*
Bloodleaf	*Iresine herbstii*
Bold grape ivy	*Cissus rhombifolia* 'Mandaiana'
Boston fern	*Nephrolepis exaltata* 'Bostoniensis'
Bottle palm	*Beaucarnea recurvata*
Bowstring hemp	*Sansevieria trifasciata*
Brilliant star	*Kalanchoe blossfeldiana*
Buddhist pine	*Podocarpus macrophyllus*
Burro's tail	*Sedum morganianum*
Butterfly palm	*Chrysalidocarpus lutescens*
Cast iron plant	*Aspidistra elatior*
Century plant	*Agave* (see Succulents)
Ceylon creeper	*Epipremnum aureum*
Chain plant	*Tradescantia*
Chicken gizzard plant	*Iresine herbstii*
Chinese evergreen	*Aglaonema*
Chinese jade	*Crassula arborescens*
Chinese lantern plant	*Ceropegia woodii*
Christmas cactus	*Schlumbergera*
Climbing fig	*Ficus radicans*
Climbing figleaf palm	*Fatsia japonica*
Corn plant	*Dracaena fragrans*
Crab cactus	*Schlumbergera*
Creeping Charlie	*Plectranthus australis*
Creeping fig	*Ficus pumila*
Creeping fig	*Ficus radicans*
Crisped blue fern	*Polypodium aureum*
Croton	*Codiaeum variegatum*
Deer's foot fern	*Davallia*
Desert privet	*Peperomia obtusifolia*
Devil's ivy	*Epipremnum aureum*
Devil's tongue	*Sansevieria trifasciata*
Donkey's tail	*Sedum morganianum*

Common Name	Scientific Name
Dragon plant	*Dracaena deremensis*
Dragon tree	*Dracaena draco*
Dumb cane	*Dieffenbachia*
Dwarf mountain palm	*Chamaedorea elegans*
Elephant's ear	*Philodendron hastatum*
Elephant-foot tree	*Beaucarnea recurvata*
Emerald feather	*Asparagus densiflorus* 'Sprengeri'
Emerald fern	*Asparagus densiflorus* 'Sprengeri'
Emerald Ripple	*Peperomia caperata* 'Emerald Ripple'
English ivy	*Hedera helix*
False aralia	*Dizygotheca elegantissima*
False arrowroot	*Maranta leuconeura*
False castor oil plant	*Fatsia japonica*
Fan palm	*Howea forsteriana*
Fat-headed Lizzie	*Fatshedera lizei*
Ferns	*Adiantum*
	Asparagus 'Sprengeri'
	Asplenium nidus
	Cyrtomium falcatum
	Davallia
	Nephrolepis exaltata 'Bostoniensis'
	Polypodium aureum
	Pteris
Fiddleleaf fig	*Ficus lyrata*
Fiddleleaf philodendron	*Philodendron bipennifolium*
Figleaf palm	*Fatsia japonica*
Finger aralia	*Dizygotheca elegantissima*
Fingernail plant	*Neoregelia spectabilis* (see Bromeliads)
Fishtail fern	*Cyrtomium falcatum*
Flaming Katy	*Kalanchoe blossfeldiana*
Foxtail fern	*Asparagus densiflorus* 'Myers'
Friendship plant	*Pilea involucrata*

Common Name	Scientific Name
Giant inch plant	*Tradescantia*
Gold dust dracaena	*Dracaena godseffiana*
Gold dust plant	*Codiaeum variegatum*
Gold dust plant	*Aucuba japonica* 'Variegata'
Golden feather palm	*Chrysalidocarpus lutescens*
Golden hunter's robe	*Epipremnum aureum*
Goosefoot plant	*Syngonium podophyllum*
Grape ivy	*Cissus rhombifolia*
Hare's foot fern	*Polypodium aureum*
Heartleaf philodendron	*Philodendron oxycardium*
Hearts entangled	*Ceropegia woodii*
Hen and chickens	*Sempervivum* (see Succulents)
Hen and chickens	*Echeveria elegans*
Hindu rope plant	*Hoya carnosa* 'Compacta'
Hindu rope plant	*Hoya carnosa* 'Krinkle Kurl'
Holly fern	*Cyrtomium falcatum*
India rubber plant	*Ficus elastica*
Ivy tree	*Fatshedera lizei*
Jade plant	*Crassula argentea*
Japanese aralia	*Fatsia japonica*
Japanese laurel	*Aucuba japonica* 'Variegata'
Japanese yew	*Podocarpus macrophyllus*
Joseph's coat	*Codiaeum variegatum*
Kalanchoe	*Kalanchoe blossfeldiana*
Kangaroo ivy	*Cissus antarctica*
Kangaroo treebine	*Cissus antarctica*
Kangaroo vine	*Cissus antarctica*
Kentia palm	*Howea forsteriana*
Lacy tree philodendron	*Philodendron selloum*
Ladder fern	*Nephrolepis exaltata* 'Bostoniensis'
Lady palm	*Rhapis excelsa*
Little lady palm	*Rhapis excelsa*
Living stones	*Lithops* (see Succulents)
Lobster claws	*Vriesea carinata* (see Bromeliads)
Madagascar dragon tree	*Dracaena marginata*

Common Name	Scientific Name
Maidenhair fern	*Adiantum*
Manda's golden polypody	*Polypodium aureum* 'Mandaianum'
Maternity plant	*Kalanchoe daigremontiana*
Mexican breadfruit	*Monstera deliciosa*
Mexican snowball	*Echeveria elegans*
Ming aralia	*Polyscias fruticosa*
Miniature wax plant	*Hoya bella*
Mistletoe fig	*Ficus deltoidea*
Money tree	*Crassula argentea*
Moon valley	*Pilea* 'Moon Valley'
Mosaic plant	*Fittonia*
Mother of thousands	*Tolmiea menziesii*
Mother-in-law plant	*Dieffenbachia*
Mother-in-law's tongue	*Sansevieria trifasciata*
Neanthe bella palm	*Chamaedorea elegans*
Necklace vine	*Crassula rupestris*
Nerve plant	*Fittonia*
Norfolk Island pine	*Araucaria excelsa*
Oakleaf ivy	*Cissus rhombifolia* 'Ellen Danika'
Octopus tree	*Schefflera actinophylla*
Old man cactus	*Cephalocereus* (see Cactus)
Painted drop-tongue	*Aglaonema*
Painted net leaf	*Fittonia*
Palms	*Chamaedorea elegans* *Howea forsteriana* *Rhapis excelsa*
Pan-American plant	*Pilea involucrata*
Panda ears plant	*Kalanchoe tomentosa*
Panda plant	*Kalanchoe tomentosa*
Paradise palm	*Howea forsteriana*
Parlor ivy	*Philodendron oxycardium*
Parlor palm	*Chamaedorea elegans*
Parsley aralia	*Polyscias fruticosa*
Peace lily	*Spathiphyllum*
Pepper face	*Peperomia obtusifolia*
Piggyback plant	*Tolmiea menziesii*

Common Name	Scientific Name
Pincushion cactus	*Mammillaria* (see Cactus)
Polypody	*Polypodium aureum*
Ponytail	*Beaucarnea recurvata*
Pothos	*Epipremnum aureum*
Prayer plant	*Maranta leuconeura*
Prickly pear cactus	*Opuntia* (see Cactus)
Prostrate coleus	*Plectranthus oertendahlii*
Purple heart	*Setcreasea purpurea*
Purple passion vine	*Gynura aurantiaca*
Pussy ears	*Kalanchoe tomentosa*
Queensland umbrella tree	*Schefflera actinophylla*
Rabbit tracks	*Maranta leuconeura kerchoveana*
Rabbit's foot ferns	*Davallia*
Rainbow plant	*Dracaena marginata* 'Tricolor'
Red herringbone plant	*Maranta leuconeura erythroneura*
Red-margined dracaena	*Dracaena marginata*
Red-veined prayer plant	*Maranta leuconeura erythroneura*
Rex begonia vine	*Cissus discolor*
Ribbon fern	*Pteris*
Ribbon plant	*Chlorophytum*
Ribbon plant	*Dracaena deremensis*
Rosary vine	*Ceropegia woodii*
Royal Charlie	*Plectranthus oertendahlii*
Rubber plant	*Ficus elastica*
Saddleleaf philodendron	*Philodendron selloum*
Sago palm	*Cycas revoluta*
Scarlet gnome	*Kalanchoe blossfeldiana*
Scarlet star	*Guzmania lingulata* (see Bromeliads)
Screw pine	*Pandanus veitchii*
Shower of gold	*Codiaeum variegatum*
Shuttlecock	*Asplenium nidus*
Sickle plant	*Crassula falcata*
Silk bark oak	*Grevillea robusta*

Common Name	Scientific Name
Silk oak	*Grevillea robusta*
Silver dollar plant	*Crassula arborescens*
Silvery succulent	*Crassula argentea*
Snake plant	*Sansevieria trifasciata*
Snakeskin plant	*Fittonia*
South Sea laurel	*Codiaeum variegatum*
Spadeleaf philodendron	*Philodendron hastatum*
Spath flower	*Spathiphyllum*
Spearhead philodendron	*Philodendron hastatum*
Speedy Jenny	*Tradescantia*
Spider ivy	*Chlorophytum*
Spider plant	*Chlorophytum*
Spleenwort	*Asplenium nidus*
Split-leaf philodendron	*Monstera deliciosa*
Spotted laurel	*Aucuba japonica* 'Variegata'
Star cactus	*Astrophytum* (see Cactus)
Stoneface	*Lithops* (see Succulents)
Stoneplant	*Lithops* (see Succulents)
String of beads	*Senecio* (see Succulents)
String of hearts	*Ceropegia woodii*
Swedish ivy	*Plectranthus australis*
Sweetheart vine	*Philodendron oxycardium*
Swiss cheese plant	*Monstera deliciosa*
Sword fern	*Nephrolepis exaltata* 'Bostoniensis'
Table fern	*Pteris*
Ten commandment plant	*Maranta leuconeura kerchoviana*
Thanksgiving cactus	*Schlumbergera*
Thatch-leaf palm	*Howea forsteriana*
Threadleaf aralia	*Dizygotheca elegantissima*
Tree ivy	*Fatshedera lizei*
Trileaf wonder	*Syngonium podophyllum*
Umbrella plant	*Schefflera actinophylla*
Urn plant	*Aechmea fasciata* (see Bromeliads)
Velvet plant	*Gynura aurantiaca*

Common Name	Scientific Name
Walking anthericum	*Chlorophytum*
Wandering jew	*Zebrina pendula*
Wandering jew	*Setcreasea purpurea*
Wandering jew	*Tradescantia*
Wandering sailor	*Zebrina pendula*
Watermelon begonia	*Peperomia argyreia*
Watermelon peperomia	*Peperomia argyreia*
Wax plant	*Hoya carnosa*
Wax vine	*Hoya carnosa*
Weeping Chinese banyan	*Ficus benjamina*
Weeping fig	*Ficus benjamina*
Weeping laurel	*Ficus benjamina*
White flag	*Spathiphyllum*
White sails	*Spathiphyllum*
Youth on age	*Tolmiea menziesii*
Zebra plant	*Zebrina pendula*

Adiantum   Maidenhair fern
ah-dee-AHN-tum

The common name of this group of rain-forest ferns is well chosen. The overall appearance of the plant is feminine and lacy, and the individual leaflets are soft and fine to the touch, like the baby-fine hair you imagine Cinderella must have had.

If you think that anything this delicate looking must need extra care, you're right. Maidenhairs are indeed more difficult than the other household ferns—but not impossible, and so beautiful they are worth the effort.

Unlike most ferns, whose stems are insignificant, the stems of maidenhair are visible and striking. They are black or brownish black, thin and wiry looking, and the green leaves do not completely hide them. The contrast between the black stems and the bright green foliage is part of the beauty of these lovely ferns.

Maidenhair ferns grow naturally in semitropical and temperate rain forests where the humidity is high and the sunlight is filtered by the trees above. Remember those two essentials—high humidity and filtered light—and you have the key to keeping maidenhairs alive. They do well in kitchens and bathrooms, where the humidity is normally higher than other parts of the house. But even there, you'll need to increase the humidity with regular misting or a pebble tray.

Some maidenhairs have the unnerving habit of dropping their fronds in the fall. Don't panic; it's the plant's way of taking a rest. Keep watering (although less often), and in about a month new shoots will begin to show.

There are many species and subspecies, all with the same general care needs.

Humidity   High, as high as you can get it. Keep a spray bottle near the plant, and spritz it often.

Water   The soil should always be lightly damp; never let it dry completely.

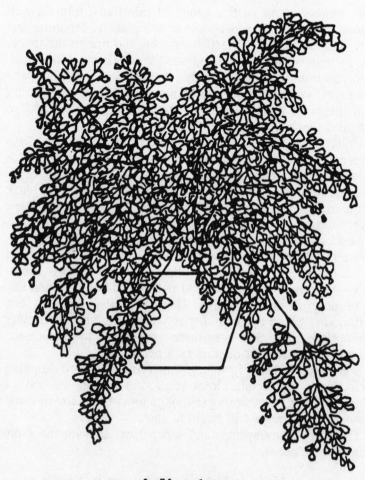

Adiantum

Temperature Will do best in a location that gets coolish (60 degrees or so) at night, say in a room that you don't heat as much as others or near a window. However, be careful not to let the fronds touch the windowpane.

Light North or east window; filtered light. Will even grow in shady corners. *Not* in full sunlight; you just have to look at the delicate leaves to know that direct sun will kill this tender plant.

Propagation Division, every three years or so.

Problems Brown tips mean it's not getting enough humidity. Don't put near a door; this plant cannot tolerate drafts.

Aglaonema
ag-lay-oh-NEE-mah

Chinese evergreen
Painted drop-tongue

The Chinese evergreen is a wonderful plant to have in your repertoire, especially if you think you have a brown thumb. You can place it almost anywhere and do almost anything to it, and it will continue to thrive. It will grow in any kind of light except hot, direct sun; it's not fussy about humidity; it won't need pruning for a very long time; and it grows slowly, so you won't have to worry about repotting for several years. All in all, a wonderful choice for people who enjoy having beautiful plants in their home but don't particularly like fussing with them.

In addition to toughness, the Chinese evergreen offers graceful beauty. Long, dark green leaves are often splashed with gray-green, white, silvery, or cream-colored markings. Several varieties are available; the primary difference is in the leaf coloration.

This plant grows naturally in humid jungly areas of Asia: the Philippines, Borneo, Indonesia, Thailand, and, as you might guess, China. Indoors, the plant stays compact and nicely shaped for a long time, but its style of growth is tall and upright, and eventually the lower leaves die off.

When it begins to look scraggly to you, cut off the stem about midway and put the cutting in water. The cutting will root in a few weeks, and if you continue to water the original plant, the stem will also sprout new growth. Often the pot you originally bought at the plant store has several plants in it, so you can let some grow tall and prune back others. When your cutting is rooted, you can either put it back in the original pot to fill in the gaps, or start a new pot. Or you can just leave it in the water; it will grow there quite happily.

Because it is so resilient, this is a very popular plant for indoor shopping malls and lobbies of office buildings.

Aglaonema

Humidity	Will tolerate almost any conditions; but will thank you for a periodic spritz from the spray bottle.
Water	Keep soil lightly damp.
Temperature	Normal home temperature is fine; this plant doesn't like to get cold, so don't keep it where the temperature drops below 60 degrees.
Light	North or east exposure is fine; anything but hot sun. Very tolerant of all kinds of light conditions.
Propagation	Stem cuttings whenever plant begins to get too tall; division when pot is quite full.
Problems	Some varieties of Chinese evergreen drip a light sap off the tips of their leaves (this explains its second common name), and this sap can damage wooden furniture.
Special features	Grows in a glass of water.

Araucaria excelsa   Norfolk Island pine
ah-roh-CARRY-ah ex-SELL-sah

It's not a true pine (although it's a cousin), but it really is a
tree, and it really comes from Norfolk Island—an island in
the South Pacific near New Zealand that has a very interesting
history.

Remember the movie *Mutiny on the Bounty*? Did you know
that it's a true story? After they set Captain Bligh and eighteen
nonmutineers adrift in a small boat, Fletcher Christian and
nine of the mutineers, along with nineteen Polynesian men and
women, landed on Pitcairn Island in the South Pacific, and
settled a colony there in 1789. Sixty-seven years later, 194
people from Pitcairn Island—descendants of the mutineers—
moved to Norfolk Island, and some of their descendants live
there still. (Captain Bligh, by the way, lived to sail again; see
Philodendron oxycardium.)

About eighty years before the mutineer families arrived,
Norfolk Island was discovered by Captain Cook on one of his
voyages through the Pacific. He found the island covered with
beautiful tall evergreens and brought specimens back to England. It was—you guessed it—the plant we know today as
Norfolk Island pine.

What we buy as a houseplant is actually a baby tree; if it
were grown outdoors, it would eventually reach well over 100
feet. Luckily, indoors it's a very slow grower, so you won't
have to worry about it hitting your ceiling.

This is not a particularly demanding houseplant; it prefers
temperatures on the cool side and enjoys high humidity but
will do with less. Your biggest problem may be finding a nice
spot for it. The key attraction of the plant is its shape and
growth habit: a set of branches grow in a circle around the
stem and reach straight out horizontally. To keep the nice symmetrical shape, place the plant far enough away from a wall
that the growing branches don't run into it.

This plant benefits from a visit outdoors in the summer
months; keep it lightly shaded.

Araucaria excelsa

Humidity	Will tolerate normal house humidity but actually likes more. While your tree is still small, keep it on a pebble tray. Otherwise, it will be happy with a misting spray now and then.
Water	Water when the top soil layer is dry.
Temperature	Will do best in a somewhat cool location.
Light	Good filtered light is best; avoid direct sun.
Propagation	You won't need to worry about pruning, and you really don't want to spoil the shape by taking cuttings, so propagation isn't an issue.
Problems	If it loses lots of needles, the plant is probably too warm.
Special features	Makes a lovely small Christmas tree, one you can use over and over again.

Asparagus densiflorus 'Sprengeri'   Asparagus fern
asparagus (like the vegetable)   Emerald fern
dense-ee-FLOOR-us   Emerald feather
SPRING-er-eye

We call them asparagus ferns, but they're not really ferns. They are, however, related to the vegetable asparagus. If you've ever seen asparagus growing in someone's garden in the summertime, after the harvest, you will recognize the look of these lacy houseplants.

The needles of this plant are soft and a bright apple green; the overall look is fluffy and feathery. The young stems grow straight up but soon arch downward. They will grow three or four feet long, and make very beautiful hanging baskets.

Asparagus ferns are quite tough houseplants. They don't need constant humidity like true ferns, and they're not finicky about temperature. Their thick roots store water, so it isn't a tragedy if you forget to water. They will live in medium light conditions, but prefer bright light. In good light, they produce tiny white flowers that are followed by bright red berries.

———————————— ————————————

Green Thumb Tip
Each individual frond (stem) has a limited life span; trim out the older, yellow stems to keep the new growth coming.

———————————— ————————————

Other Varieties
There are many varieties of the asparagus genus, and a dozen or so are sold as houseplants. All need the same general care conditions as the 'Sprengeri'. Two other popular ones are described here.

Asparagus densiflorus 'Myers' has thin, delicate green needles like 'Sprengeri', but it grows in such a different way

Asparagus sprengeri

that you might not at first realize they are close relatives. The individual stems grow straight up for a long time before they bend over. They don't branch out; each frond has just the one main stem. Needles are closely clustered on the stem, so that each frond looks very much like the furry tail of a fox. In fact, this is sometimes known as foxtail fern.

Asparagus setaceus (sometimes marked *A. plumosus*) is extremely fine and lacy looking; fronds have a flat look, as if pressed with an iron. You've seen this one before: it's often used in floral arrangements and bridal bouquets because it holds up very well after being cut. Florists call it asparagus fern.

Humidity   Normal house humidity is fine.

Water   Let the soil go a bit dry, then water thoroughly. A regular watering routine is not critical to asparagus plants, but don't let them completely dry out.

Temperature   Moderate room temperature, going coolish at night, is best.

Light   Happiest in bright filtered light, but will live in dim areas.

Propagation   Divide a mature plant every couple of years (it takes a strong, sharp knife). If your plant produces berries, try planting them; they may germinate. It's a slow process, but you get a free plant.

Problems   If your fern suddenly drops lots of needles, it's probably getting too warm, or the root system has completely dried out.

Aspidistra elatior
ass-pi-DISS-TRAH ee-LAY-tee-ohr

Cast iron plant

In Victorian times, indoor plants were considered a luxury item, something that only wealthy households had. Many of the plants we enjoy today are new varieties cultivated in the past twenty or thirty years, as the pleasure of growing house-plants has spread to all parts of society. However, a few of the classics from the Victorian era have survived to the modern age, and the magnificent aspidistra is one of them.

The common name tells the whole story: this plant is so tough, it's as if it were made of cast iron.

- Don't understand fertilizers, and don't want to learn? It's okay.
- Don't want to worry about diseases? No problem.
- Hate repotting? Doesn't need it.
- Forgetful about watering? Doesn't matter.
- Don't have good light? Not necessary.

In fact, if you want a beautiful, rich green plant that you can stick anywhere and ignore—all you want to do is enjoy it—the aspidistra is for you. Well, okay, you do have to water it once in a while, but not much. It will tolerate very, very low light, and it doesn't care about temperature. Of course, if you want a thriving, luxurious plant, give it a little humidity spray now and then and fertilize regularly in spring and summer. But you can also do practically nothing at all, and it just keeps on living.

This is a slow-growing plant and won't need repotting for quite a few years. New leaves grow up directly from the soil one at a time, unfurling slowly (often at about the same time that a very old leaf is dying off).

Humidity   Likes humid areas but will take low humidity without complaint.

Aspidistra

Water   Water moderately; don't let soil get soggy. Can go without water longer than any plant except a cactus.

Temperature   Whatever you have is fine.

Light   Actually likes low light; full sun will burn the leaves.

Propagation   By division, if you really want to.

Problems   No real problems, in the usual sense, but the broad, flat leaves do seem to collect dust too fast; it's both unsightly and unhealthy. Wipe them clean regularly (think of it as your thank-you to the plant).

Asplenium nidus   Bird's nest fern
ass-PLEE-nee-um NEED-us   Spleenwort
                                          Shuttlecock

The charm of the bird's nest fern is the way it grows. The flat, smooth leaves grow out from a central core, creating a large rosette shape. Down in the center of the core, a mass of brown fibers looks like a nest; the new fronds develop from the center, and look like little green eggs before they begin to unfurl.

The fronds grow upward at an angle, getting longer as they get older; eventually some can reach two feet in length. One very pretty variety has practically horizontal growth, and the whole plant looks like a green nest.

The bright chartreuse green fronds are basically flat, although the edges are slightly wavy, giving the plant a look of gentle motion. The leaves are not scalloped or frilly, like other ferns, so that this plant looks very different from most ferns.

Botanically, however, this is a fern, and it needs the high humidity that all ferns crave. For this reason, and because of its rounded shape, this plant is perfect for a round glass bowl, planted terrarium style (see chapter 8).

If you can provide the humidity, you will have little trouble with the bird's nest, for it's a hardy little fern. It prefers bright light but will tolerate lower; like all true ferns, it cannot stand direct sun.

Humidity   High. Keep on a pebble tray, or mist regularly.

Water   Lightly moist. Do not pour water directly down into the center of the plant.

Temperature   Not fussy; will be happy in your normal temperature range as long as that's not above 75 degrees.

Light   Bright filtered or moderate light; anything but full, direct sun.

Asplenium nidus

Propagation	Practically speaking, there isn't any good propagation method. You can divide it if you really want to, but it takes delicate surgery. Or you can plant the spores (seeds) from mature plants, if you have the patience of Job.
Problems	Like many other ferns, the bird's nest can get scale; see chapter 5 for treatment.
Special features	A long summertime visit outside on a shady patio is good for this plant.

Decorating Tip

The bird's nest is very attractive displayed on a coffee table or other low spot that allows you to look down on the plant. For another nice display, put the pot on a small pebble tray inside a round woven basket; if you can find a basket that looks somewhat like a nest, you will have a very attractive piece.

Aucuba japonica 'Variegata'   Gold dust plant
ah-COO-bah ja-PON-ee-cah   Japanese laurel
   vary-GAH-tah   Spotted laurel

Aucuba is often grown outdoors as a shoulder-height shrub or hedge; it is valuable as an indoor plant because it is very hardy, handsome, and easy to grow.

The dark green leaves are colorfully spotted with yellow or creamy white dots, and the plant attains a nice bushy shape without any pruning from you.

This plant prefers cool rooms, does not demand high humidity, and tolerates a good deal of physical abuse. All this makes it a wonderful choice for office buildings that are not heated on the weekends. In your home, an aucuba is a nice choice for entranceways, because it is not affected by drafts. It also will do well in a sun-room or enclosed porch that gets cool in winter. A large, mature plant is very attractive as a room divider.

This plant adapts well to low-light conditions, although the leaf coloration will fade in very dim areas. There is a basic, unvariegated aucuba, with all-green leaves, that is even easier to grow, for it can stand extremely low-light conditions.

Humidity	Normal house humidity; light misting when you think of it.
Water	Very lightly moist; even less in winter.
Temperature	Cool; not above 65 degrees.
Light	Medium to low; will adjust to very low light, although gold spots may gradually disappear.
Propagation	Stem cuttings.

Aucuba japonica

Beaucarnea recurvata   Ponytail
boh-CARN-ee-ah ray-cur-VAH-tah   Bottle palm
                                              Elephant-foot tree

Looking for something that is both unusual and super easy to take care of? Here it is.

The ponytail plant looks a little like a palm, but it is actually a succulent plant from the desert areas of Texas and Mexico. Its main feature is the thick brown root, which looks like an overgrown bulb and sits partly above the soil; in a mature plant, the surface takes on a wrinkled look just like the foot of an elephant.

This huge root evolved as a water-storage device for this desert plant. In its natural habitat, it can go a year without rain. In your home, it can go . . . well, maybe not a year, but easily a month without watering. This is a perfect plant for people who are out of town for long periods, or tend to forget things like watering their plants.

The leaves are long, extremely thin, and arching, and grow out from the top of the big root. Even though they are actually very tough, the leaves have a delicate, graceful appearance, and the contrast with the bulky, heavy-looking root gives this plant a very unusual and dramatic look.

Like most succulents, this is a slow-growing plant. You'll never need to prune it, and it can stay in the same pot for years—another reason this is recommended as an easy-care houseplant. It actually prefers to be tight in its pot.

To help this plant thrive, treat it like a cactus: little water, potting mixture that drains well, lots of sun. But you can also grow it successfully in lower-light corners, and it doesn't need humidity. About the only thing you can do wrong is overwater it.

Humidity   Normal house humidity is just fine.

Water   Like a cactus: let the soil go dry, then water thoroughly. Can go for weeks without water.

Beaucarnea recurvata

Temperature   Lives in a wide range of temperatures, but happiest where it's warm.

Light   Likes sun but will take less without complaint.

Propagation   Not practical for home environments.

—————————————— ——————————————

Decorating Tip

The graceful leaves can grow as long as four feet. To display this plant at its best, put it on a tall stand with lots of room all around, so the leaves don't bump into anything.

BROMELIADS

Bromeliads (broh-MELL-ee-add) are a group of exotic plants with stiff leaves and astonishing, dramatic flowers. They make fabulous houseplants; they aren't difficult to grow, and they are stunning additions to your room decor. A bromeliad is one of the few plants whose natural instincts exactly fit the conditions in your home. It likes warm rooms; it doesn't mind low light; and it is used to irregular watering. When you buy a bromeliad you get a lot for your money.

"Bromeliad" is the name of an entire family (in the classification system, family is the next step up from genus), but they are described all together here because they are similar in terms of what they need from you. Most people just call everything a bromeliad, instead of using the individual genus or species name.

Actually, you've seen bromeliads all your life, even though you may not know it. Every time you go through the fresh produce section of your supermarket you pass one: the pineapple. Visualize the stiff, spiky leaves at the top of the pineapple, the part you cut off and throw away, and you have a good picture of the foliage of many bromeliads.

In a typical bromeliad, the leaves don't have stems but grow directly from a central core. They are about an inch wide, perhaps up to a foot long, and arch over from the center. The leaves grow in a tight circle, forming a hollow cup in the very center of the plant. If the plant is one that grows upright, that cup will be a vertical cavity about two inches in diameter. It looks like a vase (in fact several species are called "living vase plant") and functions like one too. In the wild, that hollow center catches rainwater; in your home, that's where you pour the water when you water your plant.

It is from this center "vase" that the flower stalk grows. (Actually, in many cases the true flower is quite small; it is the outer covering, called a bract, that has the brilliant color. In practice, though, most people just call the whole thing the flower, and so shall we.)

The flower stays on the plant for several months, so even if you buy one that is already flowering in the shop (and that's often how they are sold), you will be able to enjoy the stunning blossom for a long time. However, the flower is the plant's swan song: after it flowers, it will die. The process of dying may take a year or more, but you should know that a bromeliad will not flower a second time.

That doesn't mean, though, that you have to throw the plant away. After the flower dies, the plant will produce a baby called an offset, a small rosette of leaves at the base of the mother plant. In the wild, the decaying leaves of the mother plant provide nourishment for the baby. In the home, however, you'll want to cut the offset away from the old plant when it is about one-third the size of the mother, large enough to show its full rosette shape. Then transplant it to its own pot, and start over.

A very young plant won't flower right away; it can take three or four years before it is mature enough to produce a flower. So if you get hooked on bromeliads (and it's easy to do), you'll probably want to buy another in the interim, so you will have a constant show.

Bromeliads grow wild in the tropical jungles of Central America and South America. Most grow on trees, using their roots to hang on to the bark; that kind of growth is called epiphytic (orchids are epiphytes too). They take in water and nutrients from the air and from forest debris that collects around their roots. Often they are found in the angle where a branch meets the trunk, especially if there is any kind of indentation there; falling leaves collect in the hollow, and as they decompose they create a rich source of nourishment for the bromeliad.

In your home, it is also possible to grow the plant this way: tie it onto a piece of driftwood and pack the root area with sphagnum moss; keep the moss damp. However, most people just keep it in the pot it came in. The pot is for human convenience; the plant doesn't need it.

Caring for Your Bromeliad

- Keep out of direct sun—medium to low light.
- Keep the soil very lightly moist. Pour water directly into the cup; keep it full.
- Average house temperatures will be fine, but the plant likes extra humidity. They do well (and look nice) on a pebble tray.
- The original plant can stay in its pot its whole life, but when it's time to repot a new offset, be sure to use soil that has a lot of organic matter and that drains extremely well. Soil mixes made especially for orchids work well, if you don't want to mix your own. Actually, you don't need soil at all; commercial growers fill their pots with bark chips. The plant doesn't need soil for nutrients; it just needs something solid to sit in so it stands upright. (In truth, the plant doesn't even need to stand upright; we need for it to.)
- Fertilize lightly in spring and summer, using a complete fertilizer (one that has all three ingredients) that you have diluted to at least half strength. This goes on the soil, not in the cup.

Varieties

There are about a dozen genera commonly sold as houseplants, and many species; here are just a few to whet your appetite.

Aechmea fasciata, called urn plant, has leaves wider than most, covered with a substance that looks like talcum powder. The flower is a knockout—shaped like a feather duster, it starts out blue, then changes to soft pink.

Billbergia zebrina, like most in the *Billbergia* genus, has leaves that grow upright, with very little arch. The leaves are attractively striped (*zebrina* means "like a zebra"), but the real show is the flower: it is at the end of a long stalk that comes up from the center vase and grows taller than the leaves, then arches over. The flower stalk has many small flowers, and is surrounded by bright-colored bracts.

Guzmania lingulata, known as scarlet star, has very pretty dark green leaves that arch gracefully and present a nice contrast to the rosette of intensely colored red bracts that sit in the middle of the plant.

Neoregelia spectabilis is called the fingernail plant, and if you ever see one you'll know why: the long, graceful green leaves are tipped with brilliant red, exactly as if painted with fingernail polish.

Vriesea carinata has the very appropriate common name of lobster claws. The leaves are light green, shorter than most other bromeliads, and grow upward at an angle. Out from the leaves comes a tall flower stalk, much taller than the leaves. The bracts are orange and tightly packed on both sides of the stalk in a sort of herringbone pattern. The long yellow flowers, when they open up, curve inward toward each other, creating something that looks like a claw.

CACTUS

In some respects, cacti may be considered the perfect house-plant—you don't have to *do* anything to them (well, hardly anything). You can ignore them for weeks at a time, and they just keep on growing.

What you don't get with cactus species is large, bushy, lush green foliage, so if that's your definition of a houseplant you might be disappointed with a cactus. What you do get are interesting shapes, sometimes wonderful flowers, and super-easy care.

Cacti are New World plants, native to North and South America. They are desert dwellers, surviving poor soil, hot sun, and months without rain because they have developed ways to store water within their stems. As indoor plants, they need those same desert conditions: sandy soil, bright sunlight, and infrequent waterings.

Caring for Your Cactus

- First of all, keep it in the brightest light you can manage. If you don't have at least one sunny window, don't try to grow cacti.
- Most important, don't overwater. The soil should be either completely dry (in winter) or almost dry (in summer) before you add more water. As a practical matter, it's often hard to tell the moisture content of the soil because the thorns make it hard to reach in with your finger. Try once a month; if the plant needs more, the leaves will look slightly puckered.
- Make sure you keep these plants in soil that drains fast. If you mix your own, it should have a lot of sand. Or you can simply use the commercially prepared cactus mix.
- Cacti have shallow root systems and do well in a flat container. Often you will see several grouped together in a shallow terra-cotta container as a dish garden; this is a very attractive way to display them.
- Avoid plastic pots; they hold water too well.
- A cactus with a round shape should go in a pot that seems just barely big enough to hold it.
- You won't need to repot for quite a while, but when you do be sure to protect your hands. Either wear leather gloves, or lift the cactus from its pot using a sling of folded newspaper.
- Many species of cactus will bloom indoors, but not until the plant itself has reached a certain level of maturity, which could be as much as ten years. On the other hand, all cacti grow very slowly, so when you buy a small plant in the store, it could be several years old already. The only

way to know for sure is to buy a plant already blooming; otherwise, just enjoy your cactus for its interesting look, and any flower will be a wonderful surprise.

Varieties

The cactus family contains many genera, and each genus has many species. If you become infected with cactus fever, you'll have many, many to choose from. Here are just a few of the more common genera. (As you will note, common names of cactus plants are particularly descriptive.)

Astrophytum, the star cactus. Has several very thick segments; when you look down on it, you see a star outline. One species is called "bishop's cap" because it closely resembles the miter worn by bishops. Produces a single flower on top.

Cephalocereus is known as "old man cactus" because of the long white, wispy hairs that completely cover it. Like all cacti it grows slowly, but it will eventually get to be a foot or more in height, when the "old man" look is even more pronounced. Flowers appear out from among the hairs when the plant is old enough (could be ten years).

Echinocactus, the barrel cactus. Mature plants have a circle of flowers around the top. Good for beginners.

Mammillaria, pincushion cactus. Many, many species, all with the distinctive pincushion look.

Notocactus, called "ball cactus." Small round shapes with thorns and a single flower. Good for beginners.

Opuntia, the prickly pear cactus. In the Southwest and southern California, large species are grown as part of the outdoor landscaping. A popular small indoor species is called "beavertail," and that's exactly what it looks like. Another is called, very descriptively, "bunny ears."

In shops, you may see an oddly formed plant that seems to be two kinds of cactus stuck together, one on top of the other.

And that's exactly what it is. It's called a graft: two species cut in half and artificially grown as one plant. The bottom half is a strong plant chosen for its sturdiness; the top half is chosen because of some visual trait, either a most unusual shape or flowers.

Ceropegia woodii
sair-roh-PEE-gee-ah WOOD-ee-eye

Rosary vine
String of hearts
Hearts entangled
Chinese lantern plant

This is a small, trailing vine with very thin stems, tiny, heart-shaped leaves, and unusual subtle flowers—altogether, a frail, delicate-looking little beauty. In reality, however, it is anything but delicate. Although it may not look like it, this native of the dry areas of South Africa is a succulent, and it's almost as foolproof as a cactus. It doesn't need extra humidity, and it can withstand periods without water.

The root is a fleshy tuber that sits on top of the soil. The stems that grow out from it are almost as thin as sewing thread; it seems impossible that anything so thin could support leaves and grow two feet long. The small leaves are attached in pairs, with a lot of stem between leaf sets. This gives an airy look to the plant that adds to the illusion of fragility.

The undersides of the leaves are purple, and the tops are dark green splotched with white; if the plant is given bright light, the leaves take on a coppery sheen.

If you are able to give this plant bright sunlight, in the summer it will produce purplish flowers right at the point where leaves are attached to the stem. The flowers have a long, stretched-out shape that flares at the end. One of its common names—Chinese lantern plant—refers to the flower, but it's not like the round paper lanterns we hang outside for summer parties; actually, the flower looks more like a flashlight!

On the older part of the plant, you may find small tubers developing near the leaves; if you take a stem cutting that includes these tubers, they will root easily. Or you can simply remove the tuber itself and lay it on top of sandy potting soil.

In general, care for this plant as you would other succulents. Use a clay pot, if possible. Mix sand into the potting soil so that it drains well. Let the soil go dry between waterings. Like other succulents, the rosary vine prefers bright light, but it will

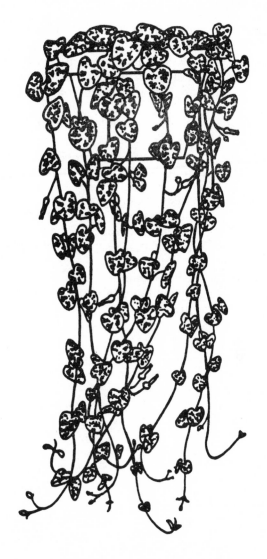

Ceropegia woodii

live in more moderate light conditions than many of its succulent cousins.

Humidity	One thing you don't have to worry about.
Water	Water this succulent lightly and carefully. Let the soil go almost dry between waterings, then drench thoroughly.
Temperature	Normal home temperature is fine.
Light	Will grow in a wide range of conditions, from bright filtered light to dim areas.
Propagation	Stem cuttings root easily, especially a section that has a small root tuber attached. The tubers also root by themselves if set on a bed of moist sand or potting soil.
Special features	Give some of the stem tubers, already planted in small pots, to the children in your life.

Chamaedorea elegans
kam-ee-DOHR-ee-ah
EL-ee-guns

Parlor palm
Neanthe bella palm
Dwarf mountain palm

This Mexican native is probably the easiest palm to grow as a houseplant. It can survive the low humidity of most homes and will tolerate quite low light. The dainty fronds look delicate but aren't; you can put this plant in a hallway or anyplace where people are apt to brush against it, with no fear of physical damage. It has an open, feathery look that nicely fills space without seeming visually heavy. All in all, an admirable choice.

Your only problem, if you have one at all, will be spider mites; the parlor palm is quite susceptible to this pest. Best solution: keep the plant clean. If you can, periodically move it outside and spray it hard with your garden hose.

This plant has one main stem, and several planted together in the same pot are more attractive than a single plant all by itself.

As palms go, it's a small plant; it won't get bigger than about three feet, and will take years to reach that height. You can even put a very small one in a terrarium with confidence that it will stay container-sized for a good while.

In plant stores you often see this plant tagged Neanthe Bella Palm. Actually, 'Neanthe Bella' is a cultivar (a cultivated variety) of *Chamaedorea elegans*; it is just like the main species, except somewhat miniaturized. Side by side, baby plants of the *Chamaedorea elegans* and *Chamaedorea elegans* 'Neanthe Bella' are very difficult to tell apart, which no doubt accounts for the confusion. If you're in the shop looking at a very small palm labeled Neanthe Bella, it may or may not actually be one. But in practice it doesn't make a great deal of difference.

Humidity   Not a critical factor; house humidity is fine.

Water   Prefers to be lightly moist.

Temperature   Tolerates a wide range of home temperatures, but prefers to be warm.

Chamaedorea elegans

Light Indirect light is best; will survive in very low conditions.

Propagation By seeds—a time-consuming process.

Problems Be alert for signs of red spider mites.

Chlorophytum
kloh-roh-FYE-tum

Spider plant
Airplane plant
Walking anthericum
Ribbon plant
Spider ivy

One of the easiest plants, and the most satisfying, the graceful spider plant will delight you with its unique growing habit. The mother plant, with long arching leaves, eventually sends out long thin stems that produce tiny white starlike flowers at the tips. Then in a few days, the flowers die off and miniature plants begin to grow where they were.

The little plantlets resemble a spider dangling from a thread, or small airplanes "flying" around the home pot. If the plant is grown in a long planter box, the young plantlets will take root wherever they hit soil, thus "walking" their way along the box or planting bed. Quite an active, energetic plant!

The roots of the spider plant are thick and fleshy, and store water well. The plant is a native of hot, dry South Africa.

One of the reasons this plant is so popular is the never-ending supply of baby plants. When little nubbins of root begin to develop on the baby plantlets, they're ready. Leaving the baby and its stem attached to the mother plant, bury the baby's root structure in the soil of an adjoining pot. When it is securely rooted (you tug gently and it doesn't come up), snip off the "umbilical cord." Even easier, just remove the plantlet; they root very easily in soil or water.

Humidity	Normal household humidity is fine.
Water	Water thoroughly, let go almost dry, water thoroughly again.
Temperature	Comfortable in warm places.
Light	Can take full sun or filtered sun; will even grow in dark areas, but less vigorously.

Chlorophytum

Propagation	Root miniature plantlets in a neighboring pot, in soil, or water. Divide the mother plant only when seriously rootbound.
Problems	The most common problem is brown tips at the ends of the leaves. For a tidier look, trim off any brown tips. Then, to prevent browning, try misting more often. And use vermiculite in your potting mix instead of perlite; the latter contains fluoride, which causes browning in some plants.
Special features	Children are fascinated by a mature spider plant with lots of "spiders." For a fun introduction to how things grow, let them cut one off and root it in their own special glass.

Green Thumb Tip

Spider plants don't generate the long runners that make baby plants until they thoroughly fill the pot with roots, so don't be in any hurry to repot. They can happily stay in the same pot, spinning out little baby plants, for several years.

Chrysalidocarpus lutescens   Butterfly palm
chris-SAL-ee-doh-CARP-us   Golden feather palm
   lew-TESS-enz   Areca palm

This beautiful palm from Madagascar is a longtime favorite houseplant. It grows to a mature height of five to six feet, but it has a delicate, feathery look that fills a large space without seeming visually heavy. The stems are yellow and the leaf fronds a bright green; the fresh colors add to the overall light look of the plant.

Several stems grow in a cluster; mature plants send up new stems from the base. These new shoots can be divided into new pots, if you wish. Or you may simply leave them in the pot; the lush foliage is a main attraction of this plant.

The butterfly, like most palms, is reasonably easy to care for. It's not one you can ignore for weeks on end, but neither is it the most temperamental plant you'll ever own. Find a spot with good light, water it regularly, mist it now and then, and it will reward you by living for a long time.

Often this is labeled *Areca lutescens* [ah-REE-cah] and called by the common name of areca palm.

Humidity   Palms are happier in humid environments, more humid than your house normally is. Whenever you have your mister out for ferns, spritz the palms too.

Water   The top layer should be very lightly moist during spring and summer; drier in winter. Don't let water collect in the tray.

Temperature Likes a room about as warm as you find comfortable.

Light   Bright filtered light; in winter, you may have to move plant closer to windows.

Propagation Divide clumps.

Chrysalidocarpus lutescens

Problems   Be on the lookout for red spider mites.

———————————— ————————————

Decorating Tip

The large size of this plant makes it ideal as a room divider or a strong accent in a hallway or entryway. Its feathery fronds make a beautiful shadow pattern on the wall or ceiling. Add a small floor light, pointing upward, so you can enjoy this show in the evening.

———————————— ————————————

Cissus
SISS-us

The *Cissus* genus is named after the Greek word for ivy. Although botanically speaking it's not a true ivy, all the species grow like ivy—a vine with tendrils that will grab onto the nearest solid surface.

Several plants in the *Cissus* genus are used as houseplants, and some of them look so different from one another that you might not realize they are so closely related. Altogether, there are more than 300 species of *Cissus,* growing in tropical and semitropical parts of the world. Some of them are succulents, about as far in appearance from their houseplant cousins as you could imagine.

The two *Cissus* species most commonly sold for indoor plants are *C. antarctica* and *C. rhombifolia*, each of which is described individually below. Others are also sometimes found, and two of them are briefly described here.

C. discolor has leaves that are much bigger than other *Cissus* species, up to six inches long; they are shaped like an elongated heart with a pointy tip. The dark green leaves have a bumpy texture and look as if someone had painted a top coat of silver gray unevenly over the green. It is called the rex begonia vine, because the leaves look much like the real rex begonia. The stems and the tendrils are red, and the undersides of the leaves are also reddish. As you can imagine, the coloration is quite spectacular. But there is a price: this one is much more difficult to grow than its cousins. You may have success if you have a greenhouse window; otherwise, stick to the easier varieties.

C. striata [stry-AY-ta] is a smaller plant with a daintier look; its common name is miniature grape ivy. Its leaf is composed of five separate segments, with the middle one being much larger, giving an overall star shape. A good choice for a hanging basket. It is not difficult to grow, just difficult to find.

C. antarctica   Kangaroo vine
ant-ARC-ti-ca   Kangaroo treebine
                                                    Kangaroo ivy
                                               African tree grape

This species of *Cissus* is native to the New South Wales area
of southern Australia—where the kangaroos live. It adapts extremely well to life indoors.

The rich green, shiny leaves are about three inches long,
and the edges are sharply scalloped, sort of like holly leaves,
although the overall shape is more like a heart than a holly
leaf is.

Kangaroo vine is easy to grow. It will live without complaint in average light, average humidity, and average house
temperature. It does best when soil is allowed to go rather dry
between waterings, so you don't have to be around to water
it every few days.

Remember, this is a vine; it will grow and grow in one long
line unless you step in. To get a full, bushy look in a hanging
basket, you'll need to keep pruning it back. It grows quickly,
and can get scraggly looking in a hurry. Root the parts you
trim off, and keep filling in the pot.

You can also allow it (or help it) to grow around a window.
Make sure the window faces north or east, or is shaded by
trees or buildings: cissus can burn up in hot sun. Add support
sticks to the pot, or build a light trellis around the perimeter
of the window, and just let the plant go. The tendrils grasp
easily. With some careful architectural pruning, you can
achieve a living curtain, with side stems reaching down and
others continuing to grow around the window. This is a very
beautiful way to screen out an unlovely view.

Varieties

A dwarf version of this plant, the variety called 'Min-
ima', has a more compact growth pattern; you'll take
care of it same as the species.

Humidity   Will appreciate misting but will survive in reg-
                  ular household humidity.

Cissus antarctica

Water   Let soil get dry on the surface, then water thoroughly; don't water again until dry.

Temperature   Survives a wide range of temperature, everything except extremely hot.

Light   Indirect light or semi-shady spots; avoid full sun.

Propagation   Root stem cuttings—which you'll have lots of, because of frequent pruning.

Problems   Spider mites are a fairly common problem. Also watch for mealybug. Biggest human problem: overwatering.

C. rhombifolia
rahm-bi-FOHL-ee-ah

Grape ivy

Grape ivy, which grows in Central and South America, isn't really an ivy, but the common name is half right: it is a member of the grape family. As a houseplant it is a very good choice for almost any home; it is such a sturdy grower that it adapts to practically any kind of conditions indoors. It is a lush and rich-looking vine that will grow even in very dimly lit areas.

Grape ivy is a vigorous climber, attaching itself with little tendrils (like a grapevine) to almost anything. It can be trained to grow around a window. You can add stakes or a small trellis to the pot, and have an essentially upright plant. Most people use it in a hanging basket, which displays the attractive leaves at their best.

The leaves are dark green with reddish bronze undersides. They grow in sets of three (actually, three leaflets make one leaf) that look a bit like poison ivy.

This plant grows strongly and quickly; if you have it as a hanging plant, prune it regularly.

Varieties

C. r. 'Ellen Danika' is a compact plant, which grows more like a small bush than a vine. Its common name is oakleaf ivy, and indeed the leaves do look like an oak.

C. r. 'Mandaiana', known as bold grape ivy, is another compact form; the leaves have the same shape as the species but are darker green, and grow more thickly on the stems.

Humidity   Normal house humidity is fine.

Water   Keep lightly moist (a bit more water than its cousin, kangaroo vine).

Cissus rhombifolia

Temperature   Normal room temperature.

Light   Prefers indirect light or light shade, but will do remarkably well even in dark areas. Don't put in full, hot sun.

Propagation   Stem cuttings.

Problems   Somewhat prone to mealybugs.

Codiaeum variegatum
coh-dee-EE-um vary-GAH-tum

Croton
Joseph's coat
South Sea laurel
Gold dust plant
Shower of gold

Crotons grow wild in tropical areas of the world—Polynesia, Malaya, Ceylon, Indonesia—and in your home they crave tropical conditions: warm temperatures, moist soil, high humidity.

Those conditions do not naturally exist in most houses, so if you are tempted by one of these beauties in the plant store, be prepared to fuss over it. However, many people are tempted, and willing to take the extra trouble, just because the plants are so striking.

The *variegatum* species is the source of most of the cultivated varieties of croton you will find for sale, although there are quite a few other species. They are widely used as outdoor shrubs in tropical parts of the country, like Florida and Hawaii.

The attraction of crotons is their foliage. The leaves come in many shapes, although generally speaking they are long, more narrow than wide, and smooth but tough, like leather. Some are shaped like giant oak leaves; some are very narrow and corkscrew twisted; some are ovals with pointed tips, like oversized laurel leaves. More striking than the shapes are the colors: green is spotted or splotched with reds, oranges, yellows, purple—and often different leaves on the same plant will have different coloration.

To keep this color vivid, crotons need bright sun. To maintain good health, they also need high humidity. They are a good candidate for pebble trays. Sudden leaf drop is a sign you need to boost the humidity.

In warm-weather parts of the country, crotons benefit from a period outdoors in the summer.

To be frank, crotons are not recommended as long-lived houseplants. They are included here because they are commonly sold around the country. Buy small ones, enjoy them

Codiaeum variegatum

as long as you can, and replace them when they die. The bright splashes of color are worth it.

Green Thumb Tip

Buy the smallest crotons you can find and plant them terrarium-style in glass bowls—the better to enjoy their fabulous color. They'll thank you for the humidity.

Humidity	Very high. Keep on a pebble tray, or spray it often, or both.
Water	Keep soil lightly moist.
Temperature	Warm. This plant is from the tropics, remember.
Light	Bright; put in your sunniest window. In the hottest days of summer, you'll need to protect from direct sun. At all other times, this plant loves sunshine.
Propagation	Stem cuttings.
Problems	Sensitive to drafts. Susceptible to red spider if air is too dry.

CAUTION

The leaves are poisonous. Don't put where small children can reach. Wash your hands after working with this plant.

Crassula argentea   Jade plant
CRASS-you-lah arr-JIN-tee-ah   Silvery succulent
                         Money tree

The word *crassus* in Latin means "thick," and so the name *Crassula* was given to this group of plants that have developed very thick leaves and stems as a way of storing water. If you remember this one thing about these plants, you will avoid the most common mistake—overwatering.

The *Crassula* genus has several hundred species, and a number of them are available for sale in plant stores and nurseries. They are all succulents, from dry areas of the world, and all have the same general growing requirements. If you see any unusual plant labeled *Crassula,* you will know how to take care of it even if you never saw it before: just follow the jade plant information.

The many *Crassula* species can be divided into two general categories, based on the way they grow. One is what we might call the "tree" species. These develop a definite trunk and branches, with individual leaves attached to the stems in a usual manner; overall, they have the general shape and upright growth pattern of a tree. The other main group grows low to the ground, and the leaves are tightly attached to the main stem in such a way that the leaf itself seems to have no stem.

The jade plant, the best known member of the *Crassula* group, is one of the tree types. It is a native of South Africa, in the rocky, dry soil near the Cape of Good Hope. It is often grown in very warm parts of the United States as an outdoor shrub.

The leaves are medium green, oval shaped, rounded on the top and flat or concave on the bottom; sometimes the edges curve under ever so gently. The common name reflects its color—jade green—and also the overall Oriental look of the plant. Sometimes this is sold under the name of *Crassula ovata,* reflecting the oval shape of the leaves.

If the plant is positioned where it gets bright sun, the leaves take on a red rim around the edges. Also, in the sun a jade

Crassula argentea

plant will bloom: clusters of small white flowers that sit upright on the stem. If you live where summers are warm, this plant will appreciate a vacation outdoors.

As a houseplant, the jade plant is extremely easy to care for. It does not need high humidity (in fact, it prefers dry air) and is not particular about temperature. It can stay in the same pot for years, and you can go out of town for a month without worrying who will water it. You can prune it or not prune it; it looks nice either way. It needs two main things: as much sun as you can give it, and lots of restraint when it comes to watering. Picture it growing in the hot, dry plains of Africa, and try to match those conditions indoors.

The leaves are fat because they store water. They also serve as a warning device to let you know when the plant needs water. When they start to dry out, the leaves look soft and feel spongy to the touch, rather than firm; when really stressed by lack of water, the leaves visibly shrivel.

It is far more likely, however, that you will have the opposite problem: too much water. It is really hard for most of us to hold off watering the way we need to. But the plant will tell you when you're making a mistake. With too much water, the plant will put out white, spiky-looking roots about one-quarter inch long at points along the stem. That's your indicator: cut back on watering.

If you want to emphasize the treelike appearance of the jade plant, prune off the lower branches and the leaves from the lower portions of the remaining branches. On its own, the plant will eventually achieve the same open look, as the older leaves die off.

If you want to make small plants to give to friends, individual leaves root easily. Let them sit on top of a small pot of sand for a few days until the end is dry and callused; then stand the leaf upright in the sand and keep the sand moist until roots begin to form. For weeks all you'll have is a rooted leaf; eventually a young plant will develop. You may also find small plants around the base of your big plant; leaves have fallen off and taken root in the soil.

Jade plants are very long-lived; many people have had theirs for ten or fifteen years, and twenty-five years is not uncommon.

Green Thumb Tip

The root structure of a jade plant is shallow, and a mature plant can easily reach a height of three or four feet. Because the leaves and stems are so thick, they are also heavy, and pretty soon the plant can become too heavy for the pot. You may need to add a few sticks to support the larger branches, and to put the pot inside another larger pot, with some pebbles as ballast.

Varieties

C. arborescens (arbor-ESS-enz) is a very pretty tree type that looks quite a bit like the familiar jade plant except for its leaves, which are more gray than green. It is also smaller and chunkier looking. It is commonly known as Chinese jade or silver dollar plant, because of the grayish color.

C. rupestris (rew-PESS-tris) is typical of the second group described above. Its leaves are squashed tight against the stem. The common name—necklace vine—gives the best sense of its appearance: this plant looks like someone took a big basketful of individual leaves and threaded them onto string for a necklace. Young stems grow upright; as they get older, they begin to twist downward, so that a mature plant has a vinelike appearance.

This is also sometimes called string of buttons; the same common names are given to several other species with this growth habit. Some of these relatives are *C. perforata* (the leaves are "perforated") and *C. perforssa*. *C. falcata*, known as sickle plant, has long leaves but the same threaded appearance.

Crassula rupestris

Humidity	Humidity is not a problem.
Water	Be very careful about overwatering. In the spring and summer, water only when soil is dry about an inch down: roughly every two weeks. In the winter, let go even drier.
Temperature	Normal home temperatures are fine.
Light	The brighter the better.
Propagation	Stem or leaf cuttings; root in moist sand.
Problems	Insects are not usually a problem, although you should be on the lookout for mealybugs.

Green Thumb Tip

Jade plants need to be in well-drained soil. When you first bring a jade plant home from the store, re-pot it. Careful, the roots are fragile. To the soil that was in the pot, mix in an equal amount of sand, and put the plant back in the same pot. It won't need repotting again for several years; this plant actually prefers to be tight in the pot.

Cycas revoluta   Sago palm
SYE-cuss rev-oh-LOO-tah

This is a most unusual-looking plant. Botanically speaking, the
sago isn't a true palm. It is a prehistoric plant, dating back
120 million years; looking at its weird trunk and exotic foliage,
you can easily imagine this plant being around during the di-
nosaur era.

The trunk is heavy, round, and covered with tough, scaly
fringe. If you took a pineapple, squashed it from the top so
that it was no longer oval shaped but round, and buried it
halfway in a pot of soil, you'd have something that resembles
the trunk of the sago.

The fronds are a very dark green, and very, very tough.
They grow in a circle around the top of the trunk; a full circle
of new fronds appears all at the same time and begins slowly
to unfurl. Indoors, it could well be two years before a new
ring of fronds develops.

This plant grows *verrrrrrry* slowly. At three years, it's still
a baby, and the foliage is feathery looking, more like a fern
than a palm. As it gets older, the fronds begin to reach their
full length (up to three feet), and the effect is more like a
palm.

Because the fronds grow all around the base, the full perimeter of a mature sago can be large: six feet in diameter is
common. The symmetrical shape is a key feature of this plant.
Be sure to give it enough room so that fronds don't bump into
the wall.

To show off the exotic look of the growth pattern, put the
pot on the floor so the plant can be viewed from above.

A frond that is cut will "live" for a long time, because the
stem holds water. For this reason, at one time sago leaves were
used in churches on Palm Sunday, and to adorn gravesites.

Humidity   Will do okay in normal home humidity.

Cycas revoluta

Water	Take it easy with water. Soak plant well, allow to become dry, then soak again. Don't let water stand in the drip saucer.
Temperature	Not particular; will take almost anything except freezing.
Light	Filtered, indirect light is best.
Propagation	Not practical.
Problems	Watch for scale.

Cyrtomium falcatum
sir-TOH-me-um foll-CAH-tum

Holly fern
Fishtail fern

The phrase "tough fern" may sound like a contradiction in terms, but the holly fern is tough in more ways than one. For one thing, the texture of the leaflets is firm and leathery to the touch. What more concerns us, this pretty plant is a tough grower.

It will take a wider range of temperatures than most plants, and will live in quite cool spots that would kill most plants from tropical areas. The tough surface of its fronds loses water vapor less rapidly than very fine and frilly ferns, and so it will tolerate normal house humidity better. And it will survive in low light. All in all, one of the sturdiest ferns you can have.

The leaflets that make up the fronds have jagged edges, much like the holly we see at Christmas. The leaves are a rich, shiny green, and the fronds grow up to two feet long, with a slow, graceful arch. The plant has an open, rather sparse look; several planted together in one pot are more attractive than a single plant.

Cyrtomiums grow in several parts of Asia. The holly fern, from Japan, is the only cyrtomium species that is widely available as a houseplant. There are others, but they are hard to find.

Humidity	Likes humidity but not so insistent as other ferns.
Water	Keep soil evenly but lightly moist.
Temperature	Normal to cool; will live in cool rooms more easily than most ferns.
Light	Moderate to low. Do *not* put in bright sun.
Propagation	By division, if you really want to.

Cyrtomium falcatum

Problems	Few. May have trouble with insects if you keep too warm or too dry.
Special feature	Incorporate this beauty into your Christmas decorations. It's as pretty as holly, and everlasting.

Davallia   Rabbit's foot fern
dah-VOLL-ee-ah   Deer's foot fern
                                                       Ball fern

In the genus *Davallia* there are several species, and on any given day in any given plant store there's no telling which you would find. However, they are all so similar in looks and care requirements, it doesn't really matter. As a practical matter, any one of them could be, and is, referred to as rabbit's foot fern.

The main attraction of these ferns is a kind of specialized root structure, called a rhizome [RYE-zohm], that all the new fronds spring from. The rhizomes grow along the top of the soil and, when they hit the edge, crawl over and start growing downward in space. They are about as thick as a pencil, and covered in fuzzy brown fibers. They are extremely strong, and furry to the touch, and feel for all the world like the foot of a small animal.

The fronds are bright green and extremely lacy. If you ever sprouted carrot tops as a kid, you'll recognize the look. (In fact, one species of davallia is called carrot fern.) They grow directly from the brown rhizomes, not from the center of the plant.

When they first appear, the fronds are very tiny and curled up in a tight spiral. The stem grows out first, with the foliage still curled up, then eventually the whole thing unfurls into a small, dainty frond. They grow out perpendicular from the rhizomes—if the rhizome is lying on the top of the pot, the fronds grow upward, and out horizontally from the rhizomes that are hanging down—and at random points on the rhizome, so the entire plant is covered with the lovely foliage.

New fronds appear often, and old ones die out continually. They start to yellow in the midsection, and then dry up. Keep these dead fronds cleared out.

The rhizomes of a mature plant can reach a foot or more in length; to protect them from banging into your table, put this

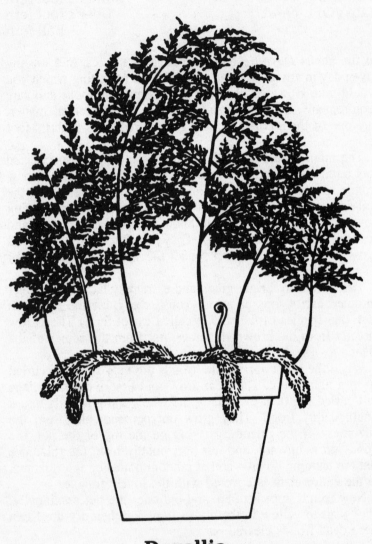

Davallia

beauty in a hanging basket. Because this is a humidity lover, line the basket with sphagnum moss and keep it moist.

In its native environment (tropical rain forests), this plant is epiphytic, which means that its roots are not down into the soil but attached to trees or other plants. It is possible to grow the plant this way at home. Sometimes they are put into a small piece of log or driftwood, hollowed out, with sphagnum moss to keep a moist environment. In fact, occasionally you can buy a piece of dried-out rhizome; soaked well and anchored to a piece of wood, it will come to life and begin to grow. The common name "ball fern" refers to the dried-up wad of rhizome.

Most of the time, though, when you find this plant in a shop it's planted in a regulation pot, and it's far simpler just to leave it there. However, this will give you a clue to the technique for starting new plants. Break off a small piece of rhizome and set in on top of moist soil or sand; pin it down with something so that it stays in contact with the soil, and keep the soil damp.

A tender fern from tropical forests needs humidity, and lots of it. Also, the top of the soil should never dry out. For both these reasons, the bathroom is an absolutely perfect spot for this plant. The shower provides lots of humidity, and the sink makes regular watering easy.

Humidity	High. Spray often. Keep in a humid room, like bathroom or kitchen.
Water	The top of the soil should always be very lightly damp; never dry out.
Temperature	Not something to worry about; tolerates a wide range.
Light	Indirect or filtered light is best. Does amazingly well in quite low light; full sun will ruin it.
Propagation	Break off a piece of rhizome, keep it moist, and a new plant will start.

Problems	Brown edges of foliage is a sign you need to increase humidity.
Special features	The fuzzy brown feet are delightful; they will make you smile every time you see them. And children are fascinated. Give them a "foot" to start a new plant from; it's a wonderful way to introduce the joy of growing things.

Dieffenbachia   Dumb cane
deef-en-BOCK-ee-uh   Mother-in-law plant

Dieffenbachias are large, splashy plants with richly variegated leaves. They are very tolerant of low light, and look handsome in large planters. They're a good choice for dim corners where you want to fill in with something green and dramatic.

Dieffenbachias are native to Central and South America, and they qualify as easy-care plants. They burn in direct sunlight, but almost any other light conditions except pitch dark are fine. They like humidity, but are less finicky about this than, say, ferns. They don't need constant watering; in fact, they do better on the dry side.

There's just one problem: the plant is poisonous. The common name "dumb cane" refers to the effect caused by its toxic juices. If you chew on a piece of leaf, or put your fingers in your mouth after working with the plant, your tongue will become swollen and inflamed, and your vocal cords will be paralyzed; you will be temporarily "dumb." Probably you wouldn't chew on a leaf—but a toddler might. And it's easy to absentmindedly lick your finger without even being aware of it. The effect lasts only a day or so, but it is quite painful.

This doesn't mean you shouldn't own dieffenbachias, just that you should be careful. If you have small children, keep the plant where they can't reach it, or wait till they are older to purchase one. And whenever you dust the plant, or do any work with it, wash your hands thoroughly. If you have a cut on your hands, wear plastic gloves.

CAUTION
The sap of this plant is poisonous. Not fatal, but painful. Don't have one within reach of small children or pets. Don't put your fingers near mouth or eyes after working with the plant.

Dieffenbachia

Actually, there is one other problem. Dieffenbachias have just one stem, and continue to grow upward. If you prune out the top part of the stem, the plant won't branch but will just replace the single stem. A mature plant can reach four or five feet in height, and by that time it has lost most of its lower leaves, leaving just a few leaves on the very top of a long trunk. This visual effect may be pleasing or not, depending on your personal taste.

If you want to shorten a tall plant, you have two choices. You can chop off the stem at the point where you want new leaves to grow; this doesn't always work but it's worth a try. Put the part you cut off in water, and eventually it too will root, and you can either start a second plant or put the cutting back in the same pot for a layered look.

The other choice is the propagation method known as air layering (see chapter 7). It's unsightly for a few weeks, but it does work. Some people think it's easier than rooting a stem cutting; some think it's harder.

All dieffenbachias have large dark green leaves, splotched and spattered with lighter colors: white, cream, or pale green. In plant shops and nurseries you will find several different species. The only difference is in the coloration of the leaves. All need the same kind of care.

Humidity   Moderate; will tolerate dry air but prefers a more humid atmosphere. Misting will be appreciated.

Water   It's easy to overwater this plant, because it's so big and lush looking. The soil should go nearly dry between waterings.

Temperature   Moderate to warm; doesn't do well in very cold rooms.

Light   Anything but direct sunlight. This plant does quite well in dim areas.

Propagation   Stem cuttings or air layering.

Problems   Don't put this plant in drafty locations. Don't water it heavily. And don't lick your fingers!

Dizygotheca elegantissima
dizzy-GOTH-ee-kah ell-ee-
  gahn-TISS-ee-mah

False aralia
Threadleaf aralia
Finger aralia

Aralia is the name of a genus of outdoor shrubs and trees with leaves arranged like a hand with spread-out fingers. Dizygotheca is not an aralia but because of its leaf pattern was once thought to be part of that genus, hence its common name of "false aralia." The names "threadleaf" and "finger" both relate to the look of the leaves. One leaf is composed of several very thin (thread thin) leaflets arranged in a circle.

If you're looking for a rich, lush plant to fill in empty spaces with lots of green foliage, this isn't it. This plant gets tall, but never full; even when full grown, dizygotheca has an airy, light look.

The lacy, delicate foliage is the main attraction of this plant. The leaves are an unusual color: a green so dark it seems to be almost purple-black, overlaid with a bronze cast; from a few feet away the overall effect is more reddish brown than green.

False aralia grows to be a small tree in its native environment, the New Hebrides Islands in the South Pacific. Indoors, it will eventually get four to five feet high. The foliage isn't wide, so it's a nice choice for a narrow space or a corner.

As the plant grows, older leaves near the bottom of the stalk die off, leaving the lacy cluster at the top. If you don't like that look, add in younger plants to the same pot, building up layers of foliage. In nurseries, large containers of dizygothecas often have several plants together, for this reason.

Some loss of leaves is normal. If many drop at the same time, that usually means a problem with water: either you are giving it much too much or much too little. This plant doesn't do well when waterlogged, nor completely dry.

Dizygotheca likes light and humidity. Low-humidity conditions tend to breed red spider mites, and they do seem to

Dizygotheca elegantissima

love dizygothecas. Mist the plants often, and keep them dust-free; both these practices will keep the spider mites under control.

Humidity	Relatively high. Mist regularly.
Water	When soil is dry an inch or so down, drench well; let go lightly dry again before watering.
Temperature	Warm rooms are best.
Light	Bright light is preferred, but will tolerate lower light for a while. Will burn in full sun.
Propagation	Stem cuttings.
Problems	Be on the lookout for spider mites. Sudden leaf drop is probably a sign of bad watering habits.

Dracaena
drah-SEE-nah

Dracaenas may well be the perfect houseplant. They grow well in low light, don't need added humidity, and are seldom bothered by insects or disease. You don't have to be religious about watering them, and they can stay in the same pot for years. With little effort on your part, they produce lush, beautiful leaves and eventually reach several feet high, so they fill up space handsomely. When you buy a dracaena, you get a lot for your money.

Because of their size and hardiness, these are popular for lobbies and entranceways of office buildings.

Green Thumb Tip

Dracaenas don't need repotting very often; in fact, they do better when they're tight in the pot. This, combined with their tall and lanky way of growing, can produce a plant that is too tall and heavy for its pot. It looks strange, and a leaning plant (like a *marginata*) could actually fall over. Solution: put the pot inside a larger decorative container. Commercial plantings often surround one tall dracaena with smaller, lower plants, all in separate pots but grouped into one big planter.

With a few exceptions, all the dracaenas have the same growth pattern. Long, thin leaves grow from the top of a single stem, which may be several inches thick in very mature plants of some species. Lower leaves continually die off, and they are not replaced with new leaves. So an older plant, if left to its own devices, will have a very long stem with just a few leaves at the top.

This long, bare stem is a distinctive feature of dracaenas. Some people like it, some don't. A very common solution for the latter group is to add a lower plant of the same species in the same pot with a taller one.

Often in nurseries and plant shops you will see a plant with a very thick trunk, cut off cleanly at about the one-foot level, with side stems growing out at the cut point and then turning upward. (See page 305.) Or to make a taller plant, sometimes growers cut off a main stem at four or five feet high, and let new growth sprout there.

You can be sure that the top part that was cut off was later rooted and put in its own pot. A plant that is large but short, with large leaves growing close to the soil line, is the result of this kind of surgery.

Dracaenas are native to Africa, Asia, and the Pacific islands, where they grow to tree size. The name comes from the Greek word for female dragon, and in fact "dragon tree" is one of the common names for a couple of species. A number of species and cultivars are sold as houseplants. The ones described here are among the more popular.

All the dracaenas need the same general growing conditions.

Humidity   Not particular about humidity; normal house or office climate is fine.

Water   Keep slightly on the dry side; overwatering is a common mistake.

Temperature   Average house temperature.

Light   Does quite nicely in low light; ideally, would prefer bright filtered light.

Propagation   Stem cuttings work, but because the stem is so
hard they take a long time. This is a good plant
to experiment with air layering.

Problems   Brown tips on the leaves are common; don't
use perlite in your potting mix.

Dracaena deremensis

D. deremensis   Dragon plant
  der-ee-MEN-sis   Ribbon plant

This popular species is fairly slow growing but does get to be
a tall plant. The leaves are about two feet long and two inches
wide. On the species, they are dark green.

A popular variety is *D. d.* 'Warneckii', which has white and
gray stripes down the length of the green leaves. This one does
particularly well in low light.

Two other attractive varieties worth searching out are 'Janet

Craig', with glossy dark green leaves, and 'Janet Craig Compacta', which is just the same but a smaller plant that stays small.

D. draco   Dragon tree
   DRAY-coh

This one is quite dramatic: a thick trunk with branches that twist upward, with leaves clustered at the outer ends. The spiky green leaves are about two feet long and stiffer than most dracaenas.

Dracaena fragrans

D. fragrans   Corn plant
   FRAY-grunz

D. f. 'Massangeana'
   mah-SAN-gee-ANN-ah

The *fragrans* species have long, wide leaves (up to three inches wide and three feet long) that arch up and over gracefully; they look remarkably like the leaves on a stalk of corn.

The broad, flat surfaces of the leaves collect dust, which is a shame, because the shiny foliage is quite beautiful. For good looks and good health, keep the leaves wiped clean.

A very beautiful variety is *D. f.* 'Massangeana', which is just like the species except that it has a wide yellow stripe down the center of the leaves. This one is very popular.

Dracaena godseffiana

D. godseffiana   Gold dust dracaena
god-SEFF-ee-anna

This species may surprise you, for it doesn't look like the other dracaenas. It's short and bushy, and grows like a very small shrub. The leaves are much rounder than other dracaenas, and speckled with creamy white. It is often sold as a terrarium plant.

This is the only species that you can propagate by division, if you should have a mind to.

Dracaena marginata

D. marginata
   margin-AH-tah

Red-margined dracaena
Madagascar dragon tree

D. m. 'Tricolor'

Rainbow plant

Green Thumb Tip
When watering, take care not to pour water directly on the leaves; they can spot.

A truly spectacular plant, the *marginata* makes a very strong accent plant, to highlight an entryway or add drama to an empty corner.

The stems are thin (about like a pencil), and the leaves are narrow—about half an inch. The leaves are dark green, and the edges are a gorgeous magenta. A variety called 'Tricolor' adds a third color, creamy white; the common name of "rainbow plant" is appropriate.

This species, like most dracaenas, is a long-lived plant. On older plants, the stems twist and turn at odd angles, sometimes turning a sharp 90 degrees and growing horizontally for a few inches, then twisting back. This quality, together with the marginata's skinny stem and the dracaena habit of dropping lower leaves, can produce a very unusual effect: a long contorted trunk, topped with a green crown of leaves. Some, especially those planted individually, look more like a piece of sculpture than a living plant. When several are planted together in the same pot, the twisting stems can interlock in interesting shapes.

Decorating Tip

If your dracaena is old enough to have developed a twisting stem, highlight its unusual beauty with a floor light pointed upward at an angle. The shadow pattern on the wall will complement the sculptural look of the plant.

Echeveria elegans   Hen and chickens
eck-i-VERY-ah ELL-ee-gunz   Mexican snowball

Echeverias are succulents from the desert areas of Mexico. The
genus name honors a nineteenth-century Mexican artist named
Atanasio Echeverria, who specialized in botanical drawings.

Echeveria elegans is a small plant with thick leaves, a pale
gray-blue-green in color, that grow in a tight circle. When it
reaches a certain age, the plant sends out short horizontal
stems with a baby plant at the end. These new plants (called
offsets) are tucked in tight at the edge of the mother plant, just
as baby chicks huddle around the mother hen.

Several succulents have this growing habit, so if you ask
for "hen and chickens" at the plant store, you may or may
not get *Echeveria elegans*. No matter—they're all charming.

If you're able to give your echeverias plenty of sun, and if
they're no longer very young plants, you may be rewarded
with pink flowers on a stalk in the summer months.

Remember the desert environment, and you will know how
to take care of these pretty little plants: lots of sun, very little
water. Humidity is not important to them, but a soil with good
drainage is. When you're repotting, be sure to add lots of sand
to the potting mix.

You won't need to repot your main plant often, though, for
this, like most succulents, grows slowly. More likely you'll be
starting new pots for the baby plants that encircle the mother.

To help ensure that your soil doesn't get waterlogged, put
these plants in clay pots. The terra-cotta color seems to blend
well with their desert look.

The *Echeveria* genus has a number of species that are commonly available in plant shops; all need the same kind of care
described here for the *elegans* species.

For more on succulents, see the special section on page 260.

Humidity   One thing you don't have to worry about
                    with succulents.

Echeveria elegans

Water Easy does it! Wait for the soil to get dry before watering. In the summer, give more water; less in the winter.

Light Full sun; likes direct sunlight.

Propagation If your plant has "hatched" babies, cut them off from the mother and plant them separately. Or remove leaves (be sure there's a small bud attached at the end) and root them.

Special features The tiny rosettes that form around the mother plant are particularly fascinating to children; let them cut off a "baby" and plant it in a tiny pot.

Epipremnum aureum
epi-PREEM-num AW-ree-um

Pothos
Devil's ivy
Golden hunter's robe
Ceylon creeper

If you were to call this plant a variegated heartleaf philodendron, no one would laugh; in fact, most people would think you were right. But devil's ivy is not a true philodendron, even though it is closely related botanically. And the care it needs is much like the philodendron's. So for all practical purposes, it might as well be a philodendron.

That might solve the problem that scientists seem to have deciding on the appropriate genus name. For a long time this plant was called *Scindapsus aureus,* and in fact you may still find it labeled this in the plant store. Today, the *Scindapsus* genus has just one species that is commonly available as a houseplant: *S. pictus,* commonly known as silver vine, which has white splotches instead of yellow.

Then for a while it was classified as *Rhaphidophora aurea,* and you may still see that name used too. But today the vine with dark green, heart-shaped leaves spattered with yellow is generally called epipremnum.

This climbing vine makes a very pretty hanging basket, if you keep it pinched back. Or if you want a more vertical plant, add a stake or pole to the pot and the plant will climb up, using its aerial roots. Devil's ivy will also climb a trellis and can be trained to grow around a window, dangle down from a balcony, or serve as a ground cover in a big floor container.

It will be happy with the humidity level and normal temperature in your house, and it does best if the soil goes almost completely dry before you water it. It will even grow in areas with poor light, although it will lose some of its yellow coloring. All in all, this is a resilient, easy-to-grow plant.

If you grow this as a dangling shelf plant or in a hanging basket, you'll want to keep the growing ends pinched back, in order to maintain a rounded, bushy shape. The ends you prune

Epipremnum aureum

off can be rooted and planted back in the same pot; they will also live practically forever in a glass of water.

Humidity   Normal house humidity is fine.

Water   Let soil go dry halfway down before watering again.

Temperature House temperature is okay.

Light   To maintain the bright yellow coloration, plant needs bright but filtered light. Will grow in low-light areas but will gradually revert to all-green leaves.

Propagation Stem cuttings root easily.

Fatshedera lizei   Tree ivy
fahtz-HEAD-er-rah LEE-zee-eye   Ivy tree
                                        Fat-headed Lizzie
                                    Climbing figleaf palm

Fatshedera is a native of a botanist's greenhouse. This plant is a hybrid, a cross between two other plants: *Fatsia japonica* (Japanese aralia) and *Hedera* (ivy), and the genus name was invented to reflect the two parents. It was first developed in 1912 by French horticulturists.

It looks like an ivy that's trying to grow up to be a tree, hence the common names. "Fat-headed Lizzie" was no doubt someone's humorous rendition of the Latin name.

The leaves show characteristics of both botanical parents. They have the color and general shape of *Fatsia* leaves but smaller. They also very much resemble ivy leaves, but much larger—about the size of an adult's hand with the fingers stretched out. The color is a rich, clear green, and the surface is smooth and glossy.

The growing habit is also a blend of the two parents. *Fatshedera* is a climber; it starts out growing upright, with one main stem, but eventually it will need some support. You can add stakes to the pot, or you can train it to grow—like ivy— around a staircase or a window trellis.

On their own, the stems don't branch out but keep growing in a straight line, like a vine. With determined pinching, you can create a short, bushy table plant. This plant grows fast, so you'll have to keep at it.

Older plants tend to lose their bottom leaves. You can train the growing end to loop down and hide the bare areas, or— which is easier—add younger plants to fill in. You'll probably want several plants in one pot, anyway, for a single plant all by itself tends to look rather scrawny.

Another solution for a scraggly plant, which seems drastic but really isn't, is to cut the whole thing way back to just a few inches above the soil line in spring and start all over. In very short order, vigorous new growth appears. Make short

Fatshedera lizei

cuttings of the leafy part you cut off; they root very fast in water.

Caring for the fatshedera isn't difficult. It needs cool temperatures, moderate light, and isn't finicky about humidity. You don't need to repot it often, but anything that uses up this much energy growing does need regular fertilizing.

Humidity   Normal house humidity is fine.

Water   The top of the soil should be very lightly moist.

Temperature   On the cool side.

Light   Bright filtered light is preferred.

Propagation   Stem cuttings root quite easily in soil or water.

Problems   Lower leaves die off naturally, but if a lot of leaves drop all at once, it usually means the room is too hot for the plant.

Fatsia japonica   Japanese aralia
FAHT-see-ah jah-PAHN-ee-cah   Figleaf palm
                                  False castor oil plant

The aralia, a native of Japan, is a very beautiful, large, lush-looking plant—when it is planted outdoors. The small ones you will find in plant shops are very young plants; they will do all right as houseplants for a while, but they yearn to be outside in the summer.

I once bought a very small aralia, about four inches high, and tried for a year to get it to grow. Eventually I gave up in frustration and decided to throw it away. Standing at the garbage can, with the lid in one hand and the puny little plant in the other, I had second thoughts. I kicked a hole in the ground with my heel, dumped the plant out of its pot and into the hole, and pushed the soil back with my foot, muttering, "All right, you little twerp; die or live on your own, I'm not going to worry about you anymore."

That was ten years ago. The plant is now about six feet high and almost that big around—and that's after being cut back to the ground once and being frozen in an ice storm. The main stems are as big around as baseball bats and the leaves are bigger than a dinner plate (in fact I use them to line serving platters for the buffet table).

Indoors, obviously the aralia will not reach this size. But with luck, and patience, you can get yours to grow better than my orphan. The ideal situation for a larger plant is to be in a large pot or tub with wheels, so it can be moved out onto a patio or balcony in the summer months.

Fatsia is also a very good choice for entryways and lobbies of buildings that get too cool for other indoor plants.

The rich, glossy green leaves are spectacular; on mature plants they can get to be more than a foot across. They do very much resemble the leaves of the fig tree (the kind that produces the fruit we eat), which is why this is called figleaf palm, and they make a wonderful addition to cut flower arrangements.

Fatsia japonica

Humidity	Will be grateful for misting indoors.
Water	Keep soil lightly damp, a bit drier in the winter. If you put your plant outdoors in the summer, don't forget to keep watering it.
Temperature	Likes cool environments.
Light	Needs bright light but not direct sun. Outdoors, it does best in filtered shade.
Propagation	Stem cuttings.
Problems	If leaves drop suddenly, the room is too warm.

Ficus
FYE-cuss

Fig

The *Ficus* genus has more than a thousand species; they are found in many parts of the world—Asia, Africa, Central America, South America, and Australia. Included are some pretty dramatic plants.

The banyan tree is a *Ficus*; it sends down roots from all along its spreading branches. As they grow older the roots get thicker, so they are like new trunks. The tree keeps spreading, and keeps sending down roots, so that eventually there's a small forest of trunks of various sizes, all connected to the same treetop. Old banyan trees (it's one tree, or many trees, depending on your point of view) can cover an area as big as a city block. A mature tree has the effect of lots of separate rooms, and always you will see children playing hide and seek among the many trunks. In some Asian countries outdoor markets are held in the shade of the trees.

Another member of the fig group is the Bo tree, which gets to be enormous. Buddha is believed to have received enlightenment while resting in the shade of a Bo tree. And another member is the shrubby tree that produces the fruit we enjoy.

About a dozen species are used as houseplants. Three in particular are very popular—the weeping fig, the fiddleleaf fig, and the rubber plant—and they are described in individual sections. Others that you may want to consider are described briefly here.

F. deltoidea
dell-TOY-dee-ah

Mistletoe fig

This fig family member from Malaya has smallish leaves (about two inches long) and an open, twisting branch structure. It is slow growing and has a small shape; if a weeping fig is a tree, the mistletoe fig is a shrub.

At one time this plant was called *Ficus diversifolia,* a reference to its different leaves ("diverse foliage"): some are rounded, some pointy on the end.

The special delight of this plant is its tiny fruit; about the size of peas, they sit up on the end of a short stem and stay on the plant a long time. The "figs" are yellow-green, which is one reason this is known as the mistletoe fig; the other reason is its native growing habit: it lives on a host tree, the way Christmas mistletoe does.

In general, this needs the same kind of care as other ficuses, but it is thirstier: keep the soil lightly moist.

F. pumila
PEW-mi-lah

Creeping fig

Like *F. radicans,* this species is a creeper and a climber. Its tiny roots attach readily to walls, and so it is used outdoors in warmer areas as an alternative to ivy. Indoors it makes an attractive hanging basket.

If you want an upright plant, add a moss stick or some other vertical support to the pot and watch the plant climb up it. Or you can keep it compact and bushy with regular pinching and pruning. The part you pinch out can be rooted very easily in a glass of water, and you'll have new plants to add back to the pot or to give away.

The leaves are small and oval-shaped, bright green and slightly crinkly. This is a sturdy plant that needs little in the way of special caretaking. It tolerates a wide range of temperature, and pests are not common.

Sometimes you may find this plant labeled *Ficus repens* or *Ficus stipulata.*

F. radicans   Climbing fig
RAD-ee-cunz   Creeping fig

This ficus from the East Indies is so different in character from most ficuses that if you saw it growing next to, say, a rubber plant you would never believe they were closely related. The leaves are small and delicate.

This little beauty is a vinelike climber and can be trained to grow around a window trellis or in a hanging basket. You can also keep it as a compact table plant, if you keep pinching out the growing tip.

It can also be used as a ground cover in warm parts of the country. Wherever a node (the part of the stem where leaves are joined) touches the ground, roots develop, so it quickly spreads. As you might imagine, stem cuttings from a house-plant root very easily, and will grow in water for a long time.

F. benjamina
binge-ah-MEEN-ah

Weeping fig
Weeping laurel
Weeping Chinese banyan

If you've been in any office building, doctor's office, or apartment building lobby anywhere in the United States in the last fifteen years, you've seen a weeping fig. They have been the darlings of interior decorators for a long time, and justly so. This member of the fig family grows into a graceful indoor tree, and is a beautiful addition to large spaces.

In its native India, this becomes a very tall tree. In your home, if you are able to give it the conditions it needs, it will eventually reach to seven or eight feet. To keep it from banging into the ceiling, prune off the top of the main stem.

This ficus branches readily, creating the silhouette of a genuine tree. The ends of the branches droop downward, which is why "weeping" is part of the common name. The leaves are pointy ovals, dark green, shiny, and small—well, small in comparison to a rubber plant. Overall, the look of the tree is dainty; it gets tall but not overwhelming.

If you want to promote the tree look, prune off the lower branches. If you want a full, shrubby look, snip off some ends of branches and root them, then plant back in the same pot.

Ficuses don't like to be moved. Even the move from the plant store to your home will be stressful for the plant, and it will drop some leaves in protest. But of course there's no way to avoid that stressful trip, so just choose your best spot—away from a draft—and leave the plant there, and soon it will grow new leaves.

Once it is established, a ficus is relatively sturdy and easy to care for. It grows rather slowly, so if you want a tree right away, you'll need to purchase a large plant. (Warning: they're not cheap.)

This ficus can grow quite nicely when it is tight in its pot. Because of its tall, treelike shape, it may appear to be top-heavy when in fact it's just fine. To compensate for the visual imbalance, put the pot into a larger container.

Ficus benjamina

138

Humidity   Like most indoor plants, the ficus likes an atmosphere more humid than most of us keep our homes, but it will adjust to less.

Water   Careful—it's tempting to overwater these tree-like plants. Let the top surface of the soil go dry before watering.

Temperature   Average house temperature is okay, but not colder than 55 degrees.

Light   The very best condition is bright indirect or filtered light, although the ficus will make do with less. It cannot live permanently in low-light areas.

Propagation   Root stem cuttings in soil or water.

Problems   Sudden leaf drop is a sign of a drafty location or too much water.

Green Thumb Tip

The trick to keeping a ficus healthy for a long time is not to move it. Once you find a good spot, keep it there. A good spot will have medium-bright lighting but not direct sun, and will not be anywhere near a draft. If you start with a small plant, choose the permanent location, one that allows lots of room to grow, and plant your ficus there.

F. elastica   Rubber plant
ee-LASS-ti-cah   India rubber plant

The rubber plant was very popular in Victorian times, and it remains popular today, probably because it is so handsome and so easy to care for. In the jungles of Malaysia, this ficus can grow almost a hundred feet tall; indoors it becomes a big, dramatic plant that you can enjoy without a lot of work. This plant will live in poor light and will tolerate much neglect. In fact, it's hard to do anything wrong—as long as you refrain from drowning it. This toughness of character is probably why the rubber plant is such a familiar decoration in offices.

The rubber plant has a thick sap that actually was used to make rubber before the Brazilian rubber tree was discovered as a better source of latex. If you accidentally break off a healthy leaf, you will see this milky white fluid oozing out; handle with care, for it can stain floors.

The leaves are a big oval with a long point at the end; they are glossy and smooth, but tough and stiff, as much as a foot long and half a foot wide. They are a rich, dark green on top, and coppery colored underneath, with a texture rather like felt. When a new leaf appears, it is tightly curled lengthwise and encased in a bright red covering, like wrapping paper; it's at the top of the stem, very striking against the surrounding dark green leaves. After a few weeks, the wrapping drops off and the leaf slowly unfurls.

The broad, flat leaves collect dust, which is a precondition for spider mites. Every few weeks, sponge off the leaves to keep them clean and shiny.

Normally, this plant has one main stem that just keeps on getting taller. After many years, it may come dangerously close to the ceiling, in which case you whack off the top. If you're a more orderly sort, you may decide to try air layering the stem (see chapter 7) before it reaches that critical point.

Several varieties are available, with interesting coloring and variegation.

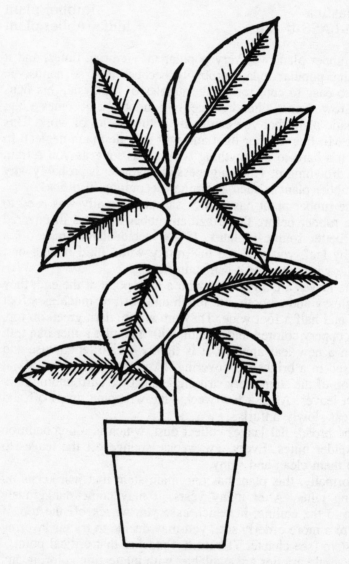

Ficus elastica

Humidity   Will do just fine in normal home humidity.

Water   Let soil go dry about an inch down, then drench thoroughly, then let go dry before watering again.

Temperature   Normal house.

Light   Tolerates low light better than most ficuses. If the plant could talk, it would ask for bright filtered light; but it will do very well in dark corners.

Propagation   Air layering.

Problems   Like its first cousin the weeping fig, this plant does not like drafts. Biggest human problem: overeager watering.

F. lyrata   Fiddleleaf fig
li-RAH-tah

The common name of this member of the *Ficus* genus refers
to the shape of its leaves. They are quite large—up to two feet
long and almost a foot wide at the widest point. The edges
are wavy, but if you could iron one flat, you would see that
it closely resembles the shape of a violin ("lyrata" means
lyre).

This is a *big* plant. It gets as tall as its cousin the weeping
fig—which is to say it will hit the ceiling—but where the
weeping fig is delicate in appearance, the fiddleleaf is heavy
and strong. The difference is in the shape and size of the
leaves: two inches compared to two feet! The leaves of weeping fig are dainty and fluttery; those of fiddleleaf are tough,
leathery, and very definitely *present*. A mature plant can seem
to fill half a room.

The plant grows with one main stem, but if you prune out
the top, it will branch. Be sure to choose a location that allows
a lot of growing room.

The general cautions about the *Ficus* genus apply here:
don't move the plant from spot to spot, keep it out of drafts,
and don't drown it. The big leaves need regular dusting.

Humidity   Normal house.

Water   Water when surface of soil is dry.

Temperature   Normal house temperature.

Light   Filtered light (south or west window) is best.

Propagation   Stem cuttings.

Problems   Loses leaves in a draft.

Ficus lyrata

Green Thumb Tip

Repotting a very big plant, like the fiddleleaf and weeping figs, is no mean trick. Fortunately, the ficuses do just fine if they are tight in the pot. You won't need to move them to a larger pot until you see roots growing out the drainage hole. In the meantime, add a layer of new soil to the top of the pot every spring.

Fittonia
fit-TONE-ee-yah

Nerve plant
Mosaic plant
Painted net leaf
Snakeskin plant

Fittonias are small, low-growing creepers from the tropical rain forests of South America. Their main charm is the beautiful markings on the small, dainty leaves. The leaves themselves are dark green, and covered all over with very prominent veins. Two species are commonly found; the difference is the coloring of these leaf veins. In *F. vershaffeltii* (vair-sha-FELT-ee-ah) the veins are red; in *F. v.* 'Argyroneura' (ar-gee-roh-NEW-rah), they are white.

Picture the fittonias growing across the forest floor in Peru: it's warm, the air is thickly humid, the soil is moist. That's what the plant needs as a houseplant: warmth, humidity, dampness. Which is about the exact opposite of most indoor environments. You can help the situation somewhat by growing fittonias in your bathroom or kitchen.

Better yet, include them in a terrarium (see chapter 8). A terrarium is an ideal environment for these humidity lovers, and they in turn are ideal for terrariums, because they stay small.

This is one of those plants you shouldn't plan to keep forever. It looks wonderful the first day you bring it home from the greenhouse; after that it's all downhill. Outside a terrarium, your fittonia will inevitably get leggy and scraggly. Pinching will maintain a nice shape for a while, but eventually you'll reach a point of frustration. Then you have two choices: give the plant a decent burial and buy a new one, or cut the stems all the way back and start over with new growth.

Humidity   Very, very high. Does best in a terrarium.

Water   Keep soil lightly damp.

Temperature   Warm.

Fittonia

Light   Bright filtered light.

Propagation   Stem cuttings root easily.

Problems   Leggy growth habit requires frequent pinching.

Grevillea robusta
gruh-VILL-ee-ah roh-BUST-ah

Silk oak
Silk bark oak

In Australia, where it grows wild, the silk oak gets to be well over a hundred feet tall. The dainty specimen we find in the plant store is an infant tree, raised from seed or from a cutting.

The plant has one main stem and an upright growth pattern—it's a tree, remember—but with careful pruning you may be able to get it to branch out. It grows rather quickly, and may reach four or five feet indoors.

The foliage is very fine and feathery, very much like a fern. As a matter of fact, often you find this in the plant store in with the ferns. Leaves are dark green with gray-green undersides.

Because of its lacy leaves, this plant is a good one to put by a window where you want to fill up space but not block the light. The plant will be happy too—it likes a lot of light.

As the plant gets older, its bottom leaves naturally die off, and nothing grows in to fill their place. So after a few years a silk oak can get to looking pretty scrawny. Many people just discard them at that point, and buy another.

The genus was named to honor C. F. Greville, who was one of the founders of Britain's Royal Horticultural Society.

Humidity	Fairly high. Keep small plants on a pebble tray. Regular misting of older plants is a good idea.
Water	Also fairly high. Keep soil lightly damp.
Temperature	On the cool side.
Light	Bright light, but not in direct summer sun.
Propagation	Stem cuttings, if you really want to try; not practical in the home environment.
Problems	Loses its leaves in very warm rooms or if allowed to dry out.

Grevillea robusta

Gynura aurantiaca
gee-NOOR-ah aw-ron-
tee-OCK-ah

Velvet plant
Purple passion vine

This plant is popular for its stunning foliage. The green leaves, and the stems too, are completely covered with very fine hairs that are bright magenta in color. From a certain angle, especially in sunlight, the whole plant is a brilliant purple.

The leaves are three to four inches long, diamond shaped, with jagged edges that curl under slightly. The purple hairs give the leaf a velvet texture, and almost no one can resist the urge to stroke the leaves.

This plant does produce flowers, but many people find the aroma unpleasant and remove the flower heads as soon as they appear.

Native to the island of Java, near India, the velvet plant is actually a vine. As a very young houseplant, it may have a small, rounded shape, but it soon grows long, trailing stems. It is much more attractive in a hanging planter or placed on a shelf, where its long stems can have room to dangle.

It can get lanky in a hurry. This is one plant you have to pinch regularly to maintain a nice shape. Even so, older plants often have a bedraggled look. If you enjoy this velvet beauty, you should probably plan to replace it every two or three years.

Or you can take several stem cuttings (they root quite easily) and pot them in the spring, for a fresh start.

It's a bit tricky finding just the right spot for your velvet plant, particularly in terms of light. The plant needs very bright light to keep its intense purple color, but direct sun, especially in summer, can burn the leaves. Probably your best bet is a south or west window that has a curtain you can close in the summer.

Humidity   Likes humid atmosphere, but don't spray it—
the leaves will spot. Keep a small plant on a

Gynura

pebble tray. Keep a hanging basket in a humid room, or line it with sphagnum moss that you keep wet. Keep your fingers crossed.

Water   The top soil should be starting to get dry before you water. Overwatering easily damages this plant.

Temperature   Normal house temperature is just fine.

Light   Bright light is essential. Direct sunbeams in summer can burn the plant.

Propagation   Stem cuttings root very easily.

Problems   Aphids seem to love this plant.

Green Thumb Tip

When you water your velvet plant, take care not to pour water on the leaves themselves. It will cause them to spot.

Hedera helix English ivy
HEAD-er-ah HEE-licks

No doubt you've seen ivy at some point in your life, so you will surely recognize this plant if you see it in the store. Only one species works well as a houseplant—*Hedera helix*—but it comes in a number of delightful varieties. Some are variegated: a mix of dark green with white, cream, or gold splotches. Some have leaves with ruffled edges. Some are almost miniatures, with tiny little leaves, cute as can be.

English ivy makes a wonderful plant for a hanging basket. Keep pinching the long, trailing stems if you want a bushy, rounded plant. Or you can train it to grow on an indoor trellis.

In offices and commercial buildings, ivy is often used in a planter on a second-story landing and allowed to hang down. You can adapt that same idea to your home by putting a planter box on the stairwell and letting it drape down, if the area is bright enough.

The main thing that ivy needs to thrive is cool temperature—actually cooler than most of us like our homes. If grown in an area over 65 degrees, ivy is very likely to attract red spider or aphids. This preference for coolness makes ivy a wonderful choice for entryways or unheated sun-rooms, and helps explain why it does so well in lobbies of office buildings that are unheated on weekends.

To help avoid insects, keep the leaves clean. If your plant can be moved, put it in the sink and rinse it thoroughly with the sprayer. Or take it outside and give it a good hard spray with the garden hose.

Humidity Moderate; will appreciate a spray whenever you have your misting bottle out.

Water Slightly damp soil in summer; drier in winter.

Temperature Cool. Over 65 degrees, you're asking for trouble.

Hedera helix

Light   Variegated varieties need bright filtered light to keep their coloration; all-green varieties can tolerate low-light areas.

Propagation   Stem cuttings root very easily, and will live in water for a long time.

Problems   Red spider and other insects are likely to attack ivy in rooms that seem comfortably warm to us; be prepared to fight them.

Decorating Tip
If you have a big plant whose pot is set down inside a floor planter, put smaller pots of ivy around the inner edges and let the stems trail over the sides.

Howea forsteriana   Kentia palm
HOW-ee-ah for-stir-ee-ANN-ah   Paradise palm
                                  Thatch-leaf palm
                                        Fan palm

Think back to the 1940s gangster movies: the detective, lying in wait in the hotel lobby, hides behind a large potted palm, peering through the fronds; as the suspect gets closer, he carefully pushes the fronds back together. That's a Kentia palm.

Or if you're not a fan of that movie genre, picture the annual concert of your son's high school orchestra; up there on the stage, off to the sides, see those tall palms? They're Kentias.

Kentia palms are the ones that used to be part of the decorations at every wedding and every dinner dance. Florists load them into vans, haul them all over town, then haul them back when the affair is over. That should give you some idea how hardy these palms are.

They're not insistent about humidity, and they do amazingly well in less than perfect light conditions. No wonder they were so popular in old hotels. Even today, it's probably the easiest, toughest palm available for growing indoors.

These palms grow naturally on Lord Howe Island, which is in the South Pacific near Australia. The genus name was chosen in honor of this homeland; the species name honors William Forster, who was a senator of New South Wales, the Australian state with jurisdiction over the island. The main city of Lord Howe Island is Kentia, hence the common name.

The seeds of this palm were brought to Europe from Australia during the Victorian era, and it quickly became a favorite for parlors of the upper classes. (In those days, houseplants were considered for the wealthy only.)

As an indoor plant, this grows slowly. Eventually it will reach seven or eight feet (tall enough to hide behind). It's one of the few palms we can grow indoors that gets to a truly dramatic size. You can't really prune it, but you probably wouldn't want to, and in any case you won't have to worry about it for a long time.

Howea forsteriana

Caring for these palms is not particularly tricky. They like filtered bright light but will live in less. They need moist soil (not soggy wet, just damp), so if you're one of those people who don't feel right if you're not watering your plants, this is a good choice for you. They'd prefer a humid atmosphere but will adapt to normal humidity levels. Overall, not a plant that needs a lot of fussing.

Humidity   Likes humid air but will do all right in normal homes. When you have your spray bottle out, give it a spritz.

Water   Keep the soil lightly moist. You don't want the roots to dry out completely. At the same time, you don't want them sitting in water.

Temperature   Warm; what feels good to you feels good to your palm.

Light   Filtered light, no direct sun. Will tolerate low light but growth slows down.

Propagation   Not practical for home environment.

Problems   Brown tips at the ends of the fronds mean you're not watering enough. Keep an eye out for spider mites.

Green Thumb Tip

Kentias do best when they are tight in the pot; if the plant looks too big for the pot, things are just right, at least as far as the plant is concerned. If it looks unbalanced to you, put the pot down inside a larger container. Baskets go nicely with palms.

Hoya carnosa
HOY-yah car-NOH-sah

Wax plant
Wax vine

Hoyas are creepers and climbers. In Australia, their homeland, they use tiny aerial roots to attach themselves to the bark of nearby trees. In your home, they will twine around any kind of support, or cling to a bark pole.

The leaves are about three inches long; they are very thick and tough, and the surface is smooth, as if someone had waxed them. There is a long space on the stem between leaves, and the leading end of the stem will be bare for a long time before leaves appear. Because of this spaciness, most people grow hoyas with some kind of support; when the stem winds around the support, the leaves seem closer together. A very common style is a wire hoop, rather like the handle of a basket.

In a hanging basket or set on a pedestal, the stems will twist downward into a stiff cascade. This plant grows like a vine, with one stem reaching toward infinity; so if you want a bushier shape, keep pruning the growing end.

The main reason for growing hoyas is their flowers: a rounded cluster of tiny, star-shaped blossoms with a sweet fragrance. Hoyas don't bloom until they are four or five years old. To encourage blossoms, be sure to:

- Give the plant lots of light; put it in your brightest window.
- Fertilize every other month except during the winter.
- Hold back on water during the winter. Let the soil go almost completely dry before watering.
- Let old flowers die and fall off by themselves. Don't remove the short stubs, because new flower buds will form there for next year.
- Keep the pot in one place while the flower buds are forming.
- Let the root system fill the pot tightly; don't be in any hurry to repot.

In the winter months, hoyas need a resting period. Stop fertilizing them altogether, and cut way, way back on the wa-

Hoya carnosa

ter. Let the soil go almost completely dry all the way down. The plant will tell you when it's time to water: the leaves will begin to pucker. Move the plant to a cooler location (still with good light, though). If you don't observe this resting period, you won't have flowers in the summer, and you will have missed the main charm of this plant.

Hoyas were named for Thomas Hoy, the head gardener for the Duke of Northumberland in the late eighteenth century. It is said that the vines were Hoy's favorite plants, and that in the duke's enormous greenhouses he gave them special attention.

Today *Hoya carnosa* is the species you are most likely to find in the plant store, although there are two other species sold as houseplants. The variegated *Hoya carnosa* is especially attractive.

Other Varieties

Hoya australis is similar to *H. carnosa,* but its leaves are rounder.

H. bella (miniature wax plant) is smaller, with narrower and more pointy leaves. Its growth pattern is tighter and more compact; the stems grow upward and then arch over. It makes a very lovely hanging plant, but it's harder to grow: it needs greater humidity and higher temperatures than most houses have.

H. carnosa 'Variegata' is just like the all-green species except for the leaf colors, which are green, pink, and creamy white, all at random: any one leaf can be a single color or a mixture of two or three colors. The new stems are pink. Even without its flowers, this is a very pretty plant.

H. c. 'Krinkle Kurl', also known as *H. c.* 'Compacta', looks very different. The leaves are tightly waved along the edges and are very densely packed along the stem, almost as if they had been threaded on. The common name of "Hindu rope plant" is not particularly descriptive but certainly entertaining.

Humidity	A bit higher than average house humidity; mist it often, or keep this plant in a humid room. A sunny kitchen window is an ideal spot.
Water	In the summer months, keep the soil surface damp. In the winter, let soil go dry. Don't let the roots sit in water.
Temperature	Warm house temperature most of the time; move to cooler spot in the winter.
Light	If you want flowers—and believe me, you do—give this plant the most light you can arrange.
Propagation	Stem cuttings.
Problems	Rather prone to mealybugs, especially if plant is not kept cool in winter.
Special features	The lovely, fragrant flowers.

Iresine herbstii   Bloodleaf
ee-riss-EE-nay HERB-stee-eye   Beefsteak plant
Chicken gizzard plant

An ordinary little plant with small leaves and a most extraordinary color—brilliant dark red; even the stems are red. It is for this color that most people choose a bloodleaf. It needs just the right spot, and its leggy growth is practically impossible to control—but the bright splash of color is worth the trouble.

The leaves are mostly rounded, but with a small notch at the end. Also, they are slightly puckered at the tip. It's as if someone had grabbed the end of the leaf and pinched out the tip, giving the leaf a twist in the process. It is this contorted shape that gives the plant its most inelegant common name, "chicken gizzard plant."

Overall, it's a smallish plant; it grows upright and will keep growing upward unless you start pinching it back, which you should do religiously. Actually, no matter what you do, after a year or so this plant will start looking really bedraggled. Your best bet is to take lots of cuttings and start a new pot.

To keep the color bright, put this plant in good sunlight.

Other Varieties

I. lindenii (lin-DEN-ee-eye) has leaves with pointy tips (no chicken gizzards).

Humidity   Average house, or a bit higher.

Water   Keep lightly moist.

Temperature   Average house temperatures are fine.

Light   Needs bright light.

Iresine

Propagation Stem cuttings root quite easily.

Problems Leggy growth. To compensate, pinch often; if it gets out of hand, start cuttings and discard original plant.

Decorating Tip

The intense red color of this plant is very attractive set against dark greens. Put a small iresine in with a grouping of other plants in a glass bowl or open terrarium.

Kalanchoe
cal-un-KOH-wee

All kalanchoes are succulents—which means that they have
thick stems and leaves (some species thicker than others) that
store water. Generally speaking, succulents grow in hot, dry
parts of the world where rainfall is scarce, and they have developed these water-holding leaves as a way of surviving long
periods of drought. To those of us who enjoy them as houseplants, this means one thing: easy on the water.

The kalanchoes are a very diverse genus (this also seems to
be characteristic of most succulents). To show you how different from one another they can be, three popular species are
described here. You will find other kalanchoes in the store, all
needing pretty much the same easy growing conditions:

> Low humidity
> Bright light
> Low water
> Normal house temperatures
> Infrequent repotting

K. blossfeldiana   Kalanchoe
bloss-feld-ee-ANN-ah   Flaming Katy
                                              Brilliant star
                                              Scarlet gnome

These kalanchoes are grown for their colorful flowers. The individual small blossoms are nothing special, but in aggregate they put on a pretty show. They are formed in clusters that sit at the end of a stalk up above the leaves, and are red, orange, mauve, pink, or yellow. A bright red-orange seems to be the most common color.

The leaves are flatter than most succulents, but tough and waxy. They are ovals, scalloped around the edges, and often there is a thin line of reddish-brown on the very edge. They are about two inches long, grow around the stem in a rosette shape, and are subtly attractive even without the flowers.

These plants show up in the stores, in full glorious flower, around Thanksgiving. To get them to bloom as holiday plants, florists have artificially put them through the environment that makes these plants bloom: short days, cooler temperatures, less water. In the natural order of things, this is what the plant experiences in its native habitat in the winter. It will then bloom in the spring.

If you buy your blooming plant in winter, you will have flowers to enjoy for several weeks. Then next year, if you want it to bloom in time for Christmas, follow these steps:

• Around Labor Day, start giving it short days. About six o'clock, put the plant in the dark; either move it into a closet, or cover it with a black plastic bag. The next morning, bring it out into the sunshine. The dark period should be at least twelve hours.
• At the same time, reduce your watering. Water just enough to keep the soil from drying out entirely.
• Small flower buds should appear in about a month. Now

Kalanchoe blossfeldiana

you can bring the plant back into normal lighting, and resume watering and light fertilizing.

• In about two more months, you should have your flowers.

If you don't do this closet routine (what horticulturists call "short-day treatment"), you should still let the plant rest in the winter; ease up on the watering, no fertilizing. Then you'll have flowers in the spring.

Some people do both: some kalanchoes are given the short-day treatment, others are left alone. That way, they have plants in bloom over many months.

While the plant is blooming, give it regular doses of fertilizer along with water. After the flowers fade, cut back the dead stalks.

You can also take the easy route and just enjoy your new kalanchoe while it's blooming this year and then buy a new one next year.

Humidity	Not something you have to worry about; normal house humidity is fine.
Water	In the spring and summer, water when the top of the soil is starting to go dry. In winter, much less water. Overall, this kalanchoe needs more water than the other species.
Temperature	Normal house temperature will do. In the winter, move to a slightly cooler location (but still with sun).
Light	To keep the plant blooming, you'll need to set it in the brightest light you can find. Direct sun is fine; only at noon in the middle of hottest summer will you need to worry about giving the plant a bit of protection from sunbeams.

Propagation   Stem or leaf cutting. Let the cutting sit bare for a few days until the cut end is dry, then root in damp sand or soil. Put the cutting in a warm, sunny spot.

Special features   The cheerful flowers.

K. daigremontiana   Maternity plant
DAY-gruh-mon-tee-ANN-ah

This kalanchoe has one main stem, encircled with long, narrow, pointy leaves. The plant is medium sized, up to about two feet high.

The leaves are very thick and tough, grayish green with purple splotches underneath and sawtooth edges. They are about six inches long, an inch wide, and the edges angle upward from the midrib. Except for the fact that the tip points downward, a leaf would look very much like a canoe.

But the real charm of this plant, and the reason people are attracted to it, is the teeny tiny plants that grow all along the edges of the leaf, in the notches. While still attached to the mother leaf, they develop roots, and then when they're good and ready they drop off and root wherever they land—in their own pot or the pot next door.

At one time it was something of a fad to take a leaf, full of babies, off a plant and pin it to a curtain. The tiny plantlets take all the nourishment they need from the mother leaf and from sunshine, but eventually the main leaf dies. It's a nice conversation piece, if you need more conversation around the house.

If you want to keep the overall plant small and compact, put it in a cool spot during the winter and cut way back on the watering and fertilizing. It will live very happily in your warm living room all year long, but in this warm environment you'll need to water more often, and the plant will grow taller.

Humidity   Your house humidity is fine.

Water   Let soil surface go dry before watering, then
                  soak thoroughly. Keep fairly dry in sum-
                  mer, even drier in the winter months.

Temperature   Warmish. Theoretically, all succulents
                  should be put in a cool spot in the winter,

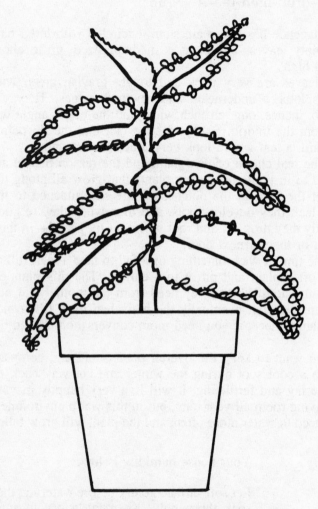

Kalanchoe daigremontiana

but these plants are so tough they don't really need it.

Light   Bright or moderate sunshine.

Propagation   Don't worry—the plant will take care of this all by itself. When the plantlets fall to the soil and get established, lift them out and repot in their own pots; you'll have thousands to give away.

Problems   None, unless it's overpopulation.

Special features Try the curtain trick if you want to. Give a leaf full of plantlets to your nieces and nephews.

K. tomentosa
toh-min-TOH-sah

Panda plant
Panda ears plant
Pussy ears

This is a small, single-stemmed plant with thick, juicy leaves covered all over with very fine hairs. The outer edges of the leaves are rimmed with brown, and the hairy surface gives a silvery tone to the basic green color.

But it is the texture that enchants. It is as soft as very deep velvet, and you cannot pass by the plant without wanting to stroke the fuzzy ears. Go ahead, it doesn't hurt the plant.

Keep this plant near your sunniest window, and remember its thick leaves don't need a lot of water.

Humidity	Normal house humidity.
Water	Let soil surface go dry before watering. In winter, water even less.
Temperature	Normal house; put it in a cooler (but still bright) spot in winter if you want to maintain small size.
Light	Bright sun.
Propagation	Leaf cuttings. Remove a leaf from the stem (be sure it has a tiny bud at the stem end), let the cut end get dry, then bury the end in damp sand.
Problems	None.
Special features	The delightful furry feel of the leaves.

Kalanchoe tomentosa

Maranta leuconeura
mah-RAHN-tah loo-coh-NEW-rah

Prayer plant
False arrowroot

If you were walking around looking at the plants for sale in the plant shop or nursery, you would almost certainly stop and admire the maranta, the plant with the very beautiful leaves. If you succumbed and bought one, you would find an extra treat that evening: the leaves do tricks.

In the daytime, the leaves stretch out horizontally, displaying the beautiful markings that marantas are known for. Then, late in the evening, the leaves angle upward and turn their undersides up. Hold your hands straight out, parallel to the floor, palms up. Now fold palms inward and touch fingertips together, as if you were praying. That's the motion the leaves make, and that's why this is universally called the prayer plant. In Great Britain it is sometimes called by the earthier name of "husband and wife plant."

The plant developed this entertaining feature as a way of conserving moisture in its native South American jungle. As the leaves turn upward, moisture on the flat surfaces runs down the stems and soaks the ground, instead of evaporating. This creates a constantly humid environment around the plant— remember that.

This is a low, spreading plant; there's a rather angular look to the way the stems grow. It looks nice on a shelf or table where the stems have room to zigzag, and it's quite attractive in a hanging basket. If you want an upright plant, you'll have to add a supporting stake to the pot.

In good light, marantas will bloom. The flower stalk is quite long (four or five inches) compared to the flower itself, which is tiny and white and shaped like a miniature orchid. Remove the stalk after the flower dies, for it just looks scruffy.

However, the main attraction of these plants is the colorful leaves. They are well-rounded ovals, about four inches long, and the flat surface between the veins feels like silk. Two varieties of marantas are commonly available (see descriptions

Maranta leuconeura erythroneura

below), and they differ only in their leaf coloration. In both cases, the undersides of the leaves echo the markings on the top sides, but in different colors, sort of like a woven fabric that shows the same pattern on both sides but with the colors reversed.

When they first appear the new leaves are very, very tightly rolled up, like extremely thin green cigars, and they stay that way for a couple of weeks, adding an extra dimension of shape to the plant.

Caring for these plants is not tricky, if you remember the need for humidity. If the leaves develop small semicircles of brown at the tip, you're not giving the plant enough humidity. While they are still small, marantas are good choices for terrariums or round bowls.

The best position in terms of light is an eastern or northern exposure, or a bright window with a sheer curtain. Direct blasts from the sun can burn the leaves, but in very low light the colors of the leaves will fade. Picture this plant growing along the forest floor in Brazil: some shade from the larger trees above, some sunshine peeking through.

The *Maranta* genus includes the plant known commercially as arrowroot, from which we get tapioca. It looks similar (and in fact is occasionally grown as a houseplant), which explains the common name of "false arrowroot."

Varieties

M. l. erythroneura   Red-veined prayer plant
air-rith-roh-NEW-rah   Red herringbone plant

The leaf has two colors of green and very striking red veins that sit on top of the leaf. Right next to the big midrib vein are squarish spots of bright apple green; next to them are larger areas of very dark green stretching all the way between the veins; then on some leaves there is an outer edge of the lighter green. Should we say the leaf is light green with dark green patches, or the other way around? It's a hard call, because leaves on the same plant will show very different proportions of dark to light green.

On the back side of the leaves, the main color is a very pale green with overtones of silver. The area that corresponds to the dark green patches on the top is a rich wine-red here on the bottom.

This is sometimes sold as *M. leuconeura* 'Fascinator'.

M. l. kerchoviana
cur-chove-ee-ANN-ah

Rabbit tracks
Ten commandment plant

These leaves are two tones of green. The main leaf color is apple green. On both sides of the midrib vein are squarish blotches of dark green, spaced regularly between the horizontal veins. They look much like the tracks of a small animal, hence the common name of "rabbit tracks." And since there are usually two rows of five, on these leaves that fold in prayer, this is sometimes called the ten commandment plant.

The foliage is less colorful than its red-veined cousin, but still quite beautiful. The undersides are pale green, and the "tracks" are red.

Humidity   High. Stand on a pebble tray, or mist regularly. Keep in a humid room. Put small plants in round bowl or terrarium.

Water   Keep lightly moist, except in winter, when you should let it get dry between waterings.

Maranta leuconeura kerchoviana

Temperature	Normal room temperature; if you're cold, the plant is too.
Light	Bright but filtered light; not full direct sun. If the leaves stay up in the nighttime position all day long, that's a sign the plant isn't getting enough light.
Propagation	Division.
Problems	Brown tips on the leaves mean humidity is too low.
Special features	The leaves that stand upright at night.

Green Thumb Tip

Marantas do well in shallow containers. Dish gardens from the florist, with several plants together in one container, often contain a maranta. Long after the other plants have outgrown this shallow home, the maranta is still thriving.

Monstera deliciosa
mon-STAIR-ah dee-liss-ee-
OH-sah

Split-leaf philodendron
Swiss cheese plant
Mexican breadfruit

It's a monster, all right. This climbing vine from the jungles of Central America will eventually produce leaves that measure more than two feet in length and almost as wide. It's a big, heavy-looking plant with a definite presence.

The main feature of this plant is its unusual leaves. After the plant reaches a certain age, it produces leaves that are very deeply notched in from the outer edges toward the center. The older the plant is, the larger the leaves are and the more deeply notched.

A very young plant has plain green leaves that look quite a bit like heartleaf philodendron, only bigger; no doubt this is the origin of the common name. But even though this is called philodendron, and in fact is closely related to it, a monstera is not a philodendron; it's a separate genus all to itself.

In its native habitat, the monstera produces roots all along the stem. The plant uses these roots to attach itself to a tree trunk, or sometimes the roots just grow down to the soil. Indoor plants have the same characteristic. On any plant except a very young one, you will see little nubbins of root structures at various points on the stem. If you want to start a cutting, get a section of stem that has one of these stubs, and you'll be amazed how quickly it forms a complete set of roots.

To promote the large scalloped leaves for which this plant is famous, put a moss-covered support stake (buy at the plant store) in the pot. That urge to climb with its aerial roots is very strong with the plant, and if thwarted it retaliates by growing only plain, unsplit leaves. Even if you don't care about leaf shape, you'll want to provide the support; the plant just grows better if it's climbing upward.

You'll find this one of the easiest plants of all. It will grow in dim corners, it will adjust to normal house humidity, and it thrives in a wide range of indoor temperatures. It's a big,

Monstera

strong, sturdy plant, and you have to work hard to do any damage to it.

Humidity	Like most plants from the tropics, it is happier in humid environment but will adapt to your normal house level of humidity.
Water	Keep lightly moist soil.
Temperature	Normal home temperature is fine.
Light	Ideally it would prefer bright filtered light but does very well indeed in low-light areas.
Propagation	Stem cuttings. Will live a long time in water.
Problems	Don't put in a drafty area.

Nephrolepis exaltata 'Bostoniensis'   Boston fern
neff-roh-LEPP-iss ex-all-TAH-tuh   Ladder fern
  boss-tone-ee-EN-sis   Sword fern

There was a time when every parlor in the United States had
a fine Boston fern in the place of honor. Then, for a time,
Boston ferns went out of style. Now, happily, they are back
in favor. Happily, because they are beautiful, elegant, and not
as difficult as you think.

"Sword fern" is the common name of several fern genera;
some are *Nephrolepis,* some not. The name describes the shape
of a frond: long and thin, wide at the base and pointed at the
tip, like the blade of a big sword. In the plant store, the only
sword ferns you are likely to find are cultivated varieties of
Nephrolepis exaltata—in other words, the venerable Boston
fern and its close relatives.

Chances are you have heard that Boston ferns are too finicky to live successfully indoors. Nonsense. Like all true ferns,
this plant is a humidity lover. The original species (*Nephrolepis exaltata*) is native to the rainy forests of the West Indies,
and even though the plants we buy now have been commercially developed especially for indoor life, the need for humid
atmosphere is still deep in the genes. But if you can provide
the humidity, you will find the Boston fern a remarkably
sturdy houseplant.

A big advantage is that this plant will live in low-light conditions. If you have a north window available, that's ideal. Or
you can keep it in a spot that gets some reflected light. Or you
can keep it in a corner that gets little light if you move it into
a brighter spot every now and then. It's perfect for a bathroom,
provided you have *some* light there and can give it enough
space.

The fronds are long (two to three feet) but flexible; at first
they grow straight up but soon start a slow, graceful curve
downward. Because of this arching growth pattern, Boston
ferns are often put into hanging baskets. They are also hand-

Nephrolepis exaltata

some on a pedestal. The one thing you don't want to do is put one where the new growing tips bang into the table.

The tip end of each frond is the part that is actively growing, and if it is physically bruised in any way it will turn brown, and soon that whole frond will die. So be sure you select a location where the tips don't grow into the wall, or where people walking by are not likely to brush against them.

In the natural course of things the older fronds will die, and new fronds grow up from the soil line to take their place. Keep the dead and dying fronds trimmed out; they will never rejuvenate, and they just look messy.

Those thin, fuzzy strings hanging down would, if the fern were planted outside in the ground, be the beginning of a new plant. The strings are called runners, and they will set new plants where they strike soil. Indoors, you can leave them dangling if you like the look, or snip them off if you don't.

In recent years some very nice varieties and cultivars have been developed. They all take the same basic care, and are different only in the look of the fronds.

Other Varieties

N. e. 'Fluffy Ruffles'. The fronds are stiff and upright, and each individual leaflet is tightly ruffled along the edges. Overall, a very frilly looking plant. This variety has a tendency to turn brown and die out in the center of the plant. The lower parts of the fronds, those nearest the soil, die, and they will never grow green there again. The outer ends still look great, though, so if you can keep the fern high (so you're not looking down on it) you can continue to enjoy it for a while.

N. e. 'Rooseveltii'. The individual leaflets on the frond are ruffled from the tip to about halfway down, then plain for the lower half. About the size of a regular Boston, but softer looking.

N. e. 'Whitmanii'. Overall, a smaller plant with a very delicate, lacy look.

And there is a compact variety of the 'Bostoniensis' that is very charming—just like the Boston, but miniature.

Humidity	High. Mist it every day, or keep in a humid room—or both. Small plants whose fronds don't droop too far can be kept on a pebble tray.
Water	Keep the soil lightly damp all the time.
Temperature	Normal house temperature is fine.
Light	Semisunny all the way to semishady; do not put in direct sunbeams.
Propagation	Division. If your aerial roots produce plantlets, you can remove them and pot them separately.
Problems	Susceptible to scale. Also, needs good drainage.

——————————— ———————————

Green Thumb Tip

If you put your Boston fern in some kind of hanging basket, the better to display its beautiful cascading fronds, don't put it so high you can't easily reach it to water and mist it. And don't forget: up near the ceiling it's hotter than down where you're standing, and plants need more watering.

——————————— ❧ ———————————

Pandanus veitchii   Screw pine
PAN-dah-nus VEECH-ee-eye

This native of the islands of the South Pacific is intriguing because of the way it grows. The long, arching leaves make a spiral around the base, each curving higher than the preceding one, exactly like the threads on a screw. Hence its common name.

And after a couple of years these plants send down aerial roots from points along the stem. In nature these roots help hold the plant upright as it gets very mature; in your house they may have the effect of pushing the whole plant up out of the soil. When that happens, it's time to repot.

The leaves are about three inches wide and three feet long, and since they grow out all around the base, they can take up quite a bit of room. They are dark green with white stripes on the sides and sharp prickles on both edges.

Older plants often look bedraggled. But Mother Nature provides a neat solution: baby plants (called offsets) develop at the base of the plant, and can be cut off and potted as a new plant. Then you won't feel bad about the old one slowly wasting away.

This plant likes to be warm and moderately humid, and if you can provide those conditions you will find it easy to grow.

Humidity	On the high side, especially in summer.
Water	Keep lightly damp in summer. Give the plant a rest in winter, with lower watering. Don't use cold water.
Temperature	Warm. Not below 55 degrees.
Light	Bright filtered.
Propagation	Offsets.

Pandanus veitchii

Problems Be careful of the sharp edges of the leaves. It's not really a problem, just something to be aware of.

Special features The roots that grow out from the stem and down toward the soil.

Peperomia
pepper-OH-mee-ah

Peperomia

The *Peperomia* genus is a big one, with more than a thousand species. The plant from which we get pepper for the table is a relative. A dozen or so species are familiar to us as houseplants; they are all small, easy to grow, have interesting foliage, and are just plain cute.

Three of the most popular plants are described here; if you find one of the others, and succumb to its charms, just go ahead and buy it. They all need the same kind of care. The only difference is the look of the foliage—and that is *very* different.

Peperomias are semisucculent plants. If you should accidentally break off a leaf someday, notice how juicy the stem is. Any plant that stores water this way needs a light hand from you on the watering can.

It also needs soil that drains well. If you make your potting mix, be sure to add a good measure of sand or perlite. Too much water plus poorly draining soil adds up to one thing: root rot, which is fatal. You're much better off giving the plant too little water (from which it can be saved) than too much (from which it cannot).

—————————— ——————————

Decorating Tip
If you want to give someone a plant for their desk, a peperomia is a good choice. It won't outgrow its space, it doesn't need a lot of water, and it isn't finicky about humidity. Just sits there looking cheerful.

—————————— ——————————

These plants produce a most unusual flower—in fact, you might not recognize it as a flower at all. What we see is a tall, thin spike, maybe four inches long, usually white, sticking straight up through the leaves. If you look very closely, you will see tiny furry flowers all along the spike.

All the peperomias stay small and compact. You will often find them included in dish gardens (several plants together in a mini-landscape in one container), and they do very well here. They are also good choices for a terrarium, if it's the kind that has an open or half-open top.

Peperomias have a very shallow root system and do well in a shallow container. That's another reason they are often chosen for dish gardens.

Humidity	Occasional misting in warm weather. Otherwise, normal house humidity is fine.
Water	When soil is dry about one inch down, water till water runs out the drainage hole. Then don't water again until dry. Even less in winter.
Temperature	House temperature is fine.
Light	Prefers filtered light or north window, but will survive in lower light.
Propagation	Leaf cuttings. Cut off a leaf and a section of stem; the roots develop at the point where the leaf is connected to the stem. Let the cutting dry out for a day before you plant it.
Problems	Overwatering leads to root rot.
Special features	The long spiky flower stalk. The unusual character of the leaves.

P. argyreia   Watermelon peperomia
ahr-juh-REE-ah   Watermelon begonia

In the art world there is a technique called *trompe l'oeil*: fool
the eye. In its broadest sense, it refers to any kind of visual
illusion.

If a trompe l'oeil artist set out to design a houseplant, it
might well be this peperomia, with its most unusual foliage.
The leaves are about an inch and a half to two inches long,
and almost as wide. They are almost completely round, and
smooth textured, and the edges curve upward ever so slightly,
creating a shallow cup. But the remarkable thing is their coloration: they look for all the world like a round watermelon,
in miniature. A leaf that looks like a watermelon? Trompe
l'oeil for sure.

Starting from the point where the stem is attached, which
is slightly off center, bands of gray curve outward and then
down toward the tip. If you wanted to draw something that
looked round, you would use that kind of curve to create a
three-dimensional effect. So even though the leaf curves inward (concave), it appears to curve outward (convex).

This species was once called *Peperomia sandersii*, and you
may find it sold under this name in some stores.

Peperomia argyreia

P. caperata 'Emerald Ripple'   Emerald ripple
cap-er-AH-tah

Once you see this plant, you will always know it. The very
dark green leaves are about an inch long, shaped like a fat
valentine, and with a very bumpy surface texture that looks
like seersucker only with taller bumps and deeper grooves.

**Peperomia caperata
"Emerald Ripple"**

P. obtusifolia
ob-TOOS-ee-FOHL-ee-ah

Baby rubber plant
Desert privet
Pepper face

The small, dark green leaves are shiny, leathery, and smooth—
no puckers here. Variegated forms are very common, with
their swirls of white, cream, or yellow mixed in with the green.

**Peperomia obtusifolia
"Variegata"**

Philodendron
fill-oh-DEN-drun

Philodendron

Chances are excellent that a philodendron—more specifically, the species known as heartleaf—is the first houseplant you ever saw. It seems that everybody's grandmother had one, and so did everybody's barbershop. In fact, because they are so very familiar, philodendrons are often overlooked. Which is a shame, because they are among the very toughest plants—easy to grow and hard to kill.

Philodendrons are native to the jungles of Central America, where they live in the shadow of the trees towering above them and where they endure rainy and dry seasons. All of this makes them incredibly tough as houseplants.

If you want to give a plant to someone who is utterly convinced that his or her thumb is terminally brown, make it a philodendron. *Anybody* can grow philodendrons. They don't care what temperature it is (as long as it's not freezing), they don't shrivel up and complain for lack of humidity, they'll survive even if you're careless about watering, and they will live in very low light. They may not thrive from all this neglect, but they won't die on you.

There are two main categories of philodendrons—those that are vines and those that aren't. In the jungle where they live, the vining types grow along the ground and then attach themselves with aerial roots to the nearest tree. (The genus name means "tree loving": *philo* for "love," *dendron* is "tree.") Like all vines, the plants in this group have just one stem, and it will grow in one long line forever unless something interferes with its growing tip.

The second group includes all the non-vines, or "self-headers," as they are called. Multiple stems come up from a central core or from a very short trunk, produce one leaf per stem, and then don't grow any longer; these plants grow wide rather than tall (or long). As the plant gets older, leaves get bigger. That is to say, the leaves produced this year, when they are all finished growing, will be bigger than last year's leaves, and next year's will be even bigger.

The vining philodendrons can be grown in a hanging basket and allowed to trail down. To have a beautiful full plant, instead of just one or two lonely vines, start your basket with several small plants and keep pruning them as they grow. The part you cut off can be rooted in water (extremely easy), and then added to your basket or used to start a new pot. You can also just leave them in water for a long time.

But what these plants really want to do is climb. Help them out by providing some kind of support. A very common sight is a philodendron pot with a moss pole (which you buy in the plant store). In the beginning you'll need to tie the plant onto the stick, but as it grows it produces small roots from the stem, which grab onto the stick. Or you can train these to grow around some kind of window trellis, even the banisters of your stairway.

The self-heading types won't climb, of course, but what they will do is get *very* big. If you buy a small, young plant, start planning where it will go when it reaches a diameter of five or six feet.

There are *lots* of philodendrons. Almost three hundred species grow wild in Central and South America, and horticulturists have been busy developing new cultivars of this sturdy genus for us to enjoy as indoor plants. Here we will meet just a few members of this handsome family; they all need the same kind of care.

Humidity	All jungle natives like humidity, but this particular group of plants has adapted quite nicely to the rather dry atmosphere most of us have in our houses. Spray them now and then if you feel like it, but it's not vital.
Water	Keep the soil just barely damp.
Temperature	Normal house temperature is fine.

Light Avoid direct sun. Filtered light or north window is ideal; will tolerate less.

Propagation Stem cuttings root while your back is turned. Will live for months in water.

Philodendron oxycardium

Vining Philodendrons

P. oxycardium   Heartleaf philodendron
oxy-CARD-ee-um   Sweetheart vine
                                     Parlor ivy

Yep, this is the one you remember from your grandmother's house. The leaves are on the small side (two or three inches long), heart-shaped, and a luscious deep green.

We have Captain William Bligh, of the *Bounty,* to thank for this houseplant. After the mutiny in 1789, when he and his loyal sailors were set off in a small boat, he sailed 3,600 miles on the open sea, eventually landing on a populated island in the East Indies. The crusty captain made his way back to England and another sailing commission, and in 1793 returned home with small vines he had collected in the West Indies— the little philodendron.

Very often we see these grown in pots with a bark or moss pole, so the vine can climb into something like an upright shape. The rather delicate look of this small-leafed plant lends itself well to a hanging basket. This one also looks especially nice growing around a window, making a kind of green valance. And because it doesn't need bright light, you can even train it to grow around the banisters of your stairway, an area that may not get much sunshine.

This plant is also sold as *Philodendron cordatum* and *P. scandens.*

P. hastatum   Elephant's ear
   hoss-TAY-tum   Spearhead philodendron
                          Spadeleaf philodendron

A number of varieties of *P. hastatum* have been developed; the principal difference is the coloration of the leaves. In the original species they are dark green, but some of the most popular new varieties have dark red coloration on leaves or stems or both. The leaves are about a foot long, and shaped like a giant arrowhead.

This species grows fast, and there is more space between one leaf and the next than is true with the heartleaf philodendron. Thus, even though the leaves are larger, this plant has a more open, airy look.

This is sometimes labeled *Philodendron domesticum.* .

P. bipennifolium   Fiddleleaf philodendron
   bye-penny-FOHL-ee-um

This is much like *P. hastatum* in size and growth habit; the difference is the shape of the leaves. Many people think it looks like a violin (hence its common name), but I've always thought it looks like the face of a young moose before you draw in the eyes and the nostrils.

Another name for this species is *Philodendron panduraeforme,* which actually seems more sensible since *bipennifolium* could so easily be confused with *bipinnatifidum,* a very different-looking species.

Philodendron hastatum

Self-heading Varieties

P. selloum
sell-OH-um

Saddleleaf philodendron
Lacy tree philodendron

A mature saddleleaf philodendron is a truly stunning plant. The dark green leaves are huge—three feet or more long—and deeply scalloped in from the edges. The long leaves are at the end of even longer stems, so the plant can extend seven or eight feet in all directions.

At the public library in my neighborhood, there is a selloum up on a ledge near a skylight. The leaves are more than two feet long and a foot and a half wide, and the leaf stalks are five feet long, so a whole leaf, from trunk to tip, is almost eight feet long. These enormous leaves are attached to a twisted thick trunk that is about six feet long; at one point a rope anchors it to the wall. Dangling from the trunk are a dozen or so aerial roots, reaching down to a length of about six feet. The plant is in an eight-inch pot, and it gets fertilized and watered once a week. No one knows for sure how old it is. It was donated to the library eight years ago, when it had outgrown a patron's house. It is a glorious sight, incredibly healthy. We all expect it to live to be a hundred.

A very similar species is *P. bipinnatifidum,* which is even bigger.

Philodendron selloum

Pilea
PILL-ee-ah

This genus of small plants is scattered around the globe, in tropical areas. Their attraction as houseplants is their unusual foliage. Different species look very different, but several have a family resemblance.

Because of their small size, and their fondness for humid atmospheres, these are very popular plants for terrariums.

Just a few of the more popular species are described here; all need the same kind of care.

Humidity	Fairly high. Likes to be on a pebble tray, and is small enough to fit nicely. Or include in a terrarium, for good humidity.
Water	Moderately damp in summer, drier in winter.
Temperature	Normal house temperature, a bit on the warm side.
Light	Bright filtered light.
Propagation	Stem cuttings root easily.
Problems	Legginess.

P. cadierei   Aluminum plant
cad-ee-AIR-ee-eye

This is probably the best known of the pileas, and it's a cutie. The leaves are oval shaped, with small blunt notches all along the edge. Their main character trait is the long patches of silvery color running the length of the leaf, as if someone had dipped them lightly in aluminum paint.

Pilea cadierei

This species in particular gets leggy. The charm of the leaf can best be appreciated when viewed from the top, so you want to keep the plant low and bushy with regular pinching. After a couple of years, even that won't be enough; the plant will just get too scraggly looking. At that point, take lots of cuttings and start a new plant.

A compact version, with leaves about an inch long, is very nice for terrariums. The original species is native to Vietnam.

P. involucrata   Friendship plant
 in-VOLL-you-crah-tah   Pan-American plant

This species from Peru has a flat, spreading look. Its leaves are ovals, an inch or so long, with a puckery surface. The dark green color is overlaid with silver and with bronze.

P. 'Moon Valley'   Moon Valley

The leaves of this species get to be about two inches, and the surface is very heavily crinkled, like seersucker only more so. The leaves are a light yellow-green with a reddish brown tint down at the base of the puckers.

P. microphylla   Artillery plant
 my-cro-FILE-ah

This species, from the West Indies, looks completely different from the others described. It grows taller and more upright, and the branching structure is more easily seen. The open, airy look is the result of the tiny leaves (*micro* means small and *phylla* means leaf).

The common name derives from an intriguing habit. In very good light, this plant produces tiny flowers that are filled with pollen, and when they are ''ripe,'' or when something brushes against them, the pollen explodes, as if shot from a cannon. Indoors you may or may not witness this phenomenon.

Plectranthus
pleck-TRAN-thus

Swedish ivy

It's not a true ivy, although it grows rather like ivy, and it's definitely not Swedish. This pretty creeping plant comes from two much warmer parts of the world: Australia (*Plectranthus australis*) and South Africa (*P. oertendahlii*). It was given this common name because it was first used as a houseplant in Scandinavia, where it is still extremely popular.

And rightly so. With its scalloped leaves and pinkish stems, and its lush growth, this plant has a cheerful look that's hard to beat. It's ridiculously easy to grow, and very attractive in a hanging basket.

In fact, this plant grows so fast you'll have to pay good attention or it will run away with you. Keep pinching it regularly, and it branches easily. If you should forget and the plant gets leggy, cut the leggy stems way back and new leaves will sprout quickly.

Meanwhile, put the cuttings in a glass of water and they'll root before your eyes. They'll also live in water for a long time, if you wish. You can also take the easy way out, and just put the snips right back in the pot without rooting them first, and most of them will set roots just fine.

Plectranthus is a member of the mint family, and a close cousin of coleus; in fact, one common name is "prostrate coleus," meaning coleus lying down. Two species are popular as houseplants. The main difference is the coloring of the leaves; they need the same kind of care.

Humidity   Your house is probably a bit too dry; whenever you have your spray bottle out, give this plant a spritz.

Water   Water when soil surface starts to go dry. If underwatered, leaves go limp but will recover.

Temperature   Household temperatures are fine.

Plectranthus oertendahlii

Light	Tolerates a wide range of light conditions; prefers bright light but will live very nicely in less.

Propagation   Stem cuttings root like *that.*

Varieties

P. australis (aw-STRAY-liss). This species, known as Swedish ivy or Creeping Charlie, is the more common. It has all-green leaves that are about an inch long, almost round, with scalloped edges.

P. oertendahlii (or-ten-DOLL-ee-eye). Known as royal Charlie or prostrate coleus, this is a more colorful version of Swedish ivy. The leaves are about the same size as the green species, but the veins are silvery white, and the undersides are magenta. This is especially pretty in a hanging basket or cascading down from a shelf, where some of the purple coloring is in view.

------------------------------ ------------------------------

Decorating Tip

In nature, this plant is a creeper, reaching out in all directions along the top of the soil. Indoors, you can use it as a kind of ground cover, to fill in the top of a large pot containing a big plant. When the plectranthus reaches the edge of the pot, it will crawl over and keep growing.

------------------------------ ------------------------------

Podocarpus macrophyllus   Buddhist pine
poh-doh-CARP-us mack-roh-FILE-us   Japanese yew

It isn't a true pine, nor is it a yew, but it really is a tree, and it is reminiscent of both those types of trees.

The podocarpus, in its original home in Asia, is a needle-leaf tree that gets to be about forty feet high. What we have as a houseplant is really a baby tree, and indoors it grows at about the same rate as a tree does outdoors—slowly.

The plant has a main stem and horizontal branches, just like the tree it is, and on an older plant the branches droop downward. The dark green needles are about two to three inches long, very narrow, and tightly packed on the branches. They look quite a bit like the foliage of a yew tree that has been fed steroids; the name *macrophyllus* means "big leaf," and for a tree with needles, these are indeed big.

Overall the plant has a lacy, feathery look and seems delicate, but it isn't. If you have a spot in your house that seems to call out for a large plant, one that can withstand drafts and less than ideal light, this is it. But if you want a big plant fast, buy a good-sized one, because a small one will take a long, long time to reach your ceiling.

This slow growth is one reason this plant is popular in terrariums. A small podocarpus, with its vertical outline, still looks like a tree compared to most other terrarium plants, and is often chosen to be the "tall" plant in a dish garden.

Often you see this plant in a large tub so it can be moved out onto a patio or balcony to enjoy the fresh air.

If you want to emphasize the tree look of your big podocarpus, do some careful pruning in the spring. Take out some of the random·side branches, to accentuate the main trunk and promote upward growth.

Humidity   Not finicky, but likes a misting now and then.

Water   Lightly moist in summer, much drier in winter.

Podocarpus macrophyllus

Temperature   Will tolerate a range of temperature from cool to warm, but not hot; likes to be cool in winter.

Light   Anything from semishady to semisunny, just not full sun.

Propagation   Stem cuttings.

Polypodium aureum
polly-POD-ium AW-ree-um

Polypody
Hare's foot fern
Bear's paw fern
Crisped blue fern

This fern from South America and Australia is hardy, easier to maintain than many other types of ferns, and has those cute "feet" that make it fun to look at.

The feet are actually rhizomes (pronounced RYE-zome), a kind of specialized stem that grows horizontally along the top of the soil. They are covered with fuzzy brown fibers, which makes them look like the paws of a furry animal, and will creep over the edge of the pot and start growing downward. If the plant is in some kind of hanging container, the rhizomes will grow several feet long. New fronds grow out from these rhizomes, curled up in a very tight ball that slowly unfurls.

So far, this might be the description of the *Davallia* ferns (rabbit's foot fern), but once the frond is fully visible, the resemblance ends. The foliage of the polypodium is quite different from the lacy, delicate fronds of the *Davallia* genus.

Individual fronds are large, some reaching three feet or more long; the individual leaflets that make up the frond are about an inch wide and five or six inches long. Their surface is smooth and feels tough, like flexible leather. And the color is very different—a bluish green that gives this fern one of its common names.

On the back side of the fronds are small dots that hold the seeds (in ferns they're called spores); these dots are reddish gold, which may account for the species name (*aureum* means gold). Or it may be that some botanist thought the fuzzy brown feet looked golden.

The fronds grow upright at first and then droop over. Since each one can be three feet long, and since they grow out from the rhizomes in all directions, you'd better find a large spot for this big plant. A hanging basket that shows off the furry feet is a good choice.

Polypodium aureum

All things considered, this is a tough fern. It isn't as foolproof as, say, an aspidistra, but as ferns go it's quite hardy. It does need plenty of water, but at least the fronds won't turn brown at the blink of an eye, and they can endure a normal amount of household traffic.

Other Varieties

P. a. 'Mandaianum' (Manda's golden polypody). This is much like the main species, except the leaflets are ruffled all along the edges, giving the whole plant a frillier look.

Humidity	Every fern enjoys high humidity, including this one; be generous with the mister.
Water	Lots. Don't let the soil go dry. But a word of caution: be sure the soil drains well, so you don't get root rot.
Temperature	Normal house temperatures are fine.
Light	Does well in moderate or low-light situations.
Propagation	Break off part of a ''foot'' and keep it in moist sand or soil till it sprouts new growth.

Green Thumb Tip

All ferns reproduce themselves in nature with seeds (called spores) that show up on the back side of the fronds as dark dots. Grown indoors, they don't always show spores, but polypodiums do.

At the same time, most ferns grown indoors are susceptible to an insect pest called scale—which shows up on the back side of the frond as dark dots.

Polypodiums seem to be less bothered by scale

than some others, but if you have other ferns that get scale, they may spread to the polypodiums.

How do you tell the difference between scale and spore cases?

- Spore cases are placed in a regular pattern; none are on stems.
- Scale will be found at random on the fronds and clustered on the stems.
- Scale is darker than polypodium spore cases and usually bigger.

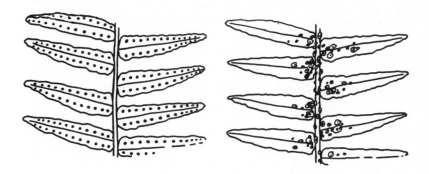

Black or brown dots on the back side of fern fronds are spore cases if they are in a very regular pattern (left) and scale (a disease) if they are all in a jumble on top of each other (right).

Polyscias
poh-LISS-ee-us

Polyscias grow naturally in Southeast Asia and the islands of the South Pacific, where they grow to be shrubs or small trees. The genus name means "many shades," which means either that it makes a good shade tree or, if the person who named it had a sense of humor, that it has a lot of leaves, each of which provides very little shade. If it grows in its natural habitat anything like the way it grows indoors, my money is on the latter theory.

This plant tends to show lots of stem, with relatively few leaves at the ends of branches. On an older plant the main stem gets gnarled and knobby, and the branches also twist and curve, so that the whole plant looks like a miniature version of the windswept trees along the Pacific coast.

It is the unusual form that endears the plant to owners. The ming aralia in particular has an Oriental look to it, and a small plant is often chosen as the centerpiece for a dish garden that its designer intends to be Japanese in feeling.

Two species are commonly available as houseplants, and they look about as much like each other as a pineapple looks like a banana. However, both need pretty much the same kind of care. And in both cases, the secret of success is the same: *don't move this plant around.* Find the spot in your house that best matches its needs—no drafts, filtered light—and leave it there.

Don't be dismayed if it drops a lot of leaves as soon as you bring it home from the store. That's its reaction to being moved, and if you don't panic, it will grow new leaves. It's not the easiest plant to grow, but many people are fond of its dramatic and unusual shape.

Varieties

P. balfouriana (bal-four-ee-ANN-ah), known as balfour aralia. The leaves are almost round, about two inches wide,

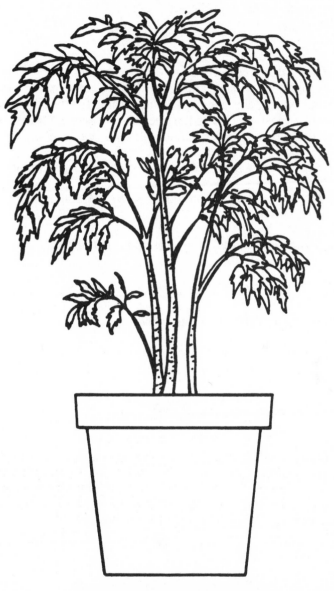

Polyscias fruticosa

and lightly scalloped on the edges. This one will tolerate low light much better than the ming aralia. There are several cultivars of the balfouriana, some variegated and some with white veins.

P. fruticosa (fruit-ee-COH-sah). In this species, called ming aralia or parsley aralia, the leaves are feathery, deeply cut and curled; the common name is apt, for they look quite a bit like parsley. This is the one that is used in Oriental dish gardens, and sometimes maintained as a bonsai plant.

Humidity   A bit higher than normal indoor humidity.

Water   Water thoroughly when the soil is dry to the touch.

Temperature   Normal house temperature. Keep away from drafts.

Light   Medium to low.

Propagation   Stem cuttings (slow).

Problems   Doesn't like to be moved around.

Green Thumb Tip

This plant stubbornly insists on staying in one place, and will drop its leaves in retaliation if you move it. One aspect of this stubbornness is actually a blessing: it doesn't want to be repotted. Wait till the roots are seriously growing out the drainage hole.

Pteris   Ribbon fern
TERRace (like the patio)   Table fern

As a group, pteris ferns are pretty sturdy—as ferns go, that is. They'll live for weeks with artificial light (one reason they're called table ferns), they tolerate dry air better than other ferns, and they can withstand a certain amount of physical contact.

The *Pteris* genus includes a half dozen or so species that are sold as houseplants, and from these many cultivars have been developed. So if you went to the plant store in search of a table fern, you'd find lots to choose from. One popular species, *Pteris cretica,* is shown here, but they all need much the same kind of growing conditions and, with a couple of exceptions, they all look more or less alike.

The pteris foliage is unusual, and unfernlike. Each frond is composed of several leaflets (usually five), each one long and narrow (like a ribbon, thus ribbon fern); the middle leaflet is much longer than the others. The whole frond looks a bit like a green starfish, and sits at the end of a long, bare stalk.

In some species the ends of the leaflets are forked, as if the leaflet started to divide into two halves but then changed its mind. It is not at all unusual for one plant to have fronds of different shapes.

The fronds originate from brown rhizomes, which grow just under the surface of the soil. They seem like roots but actually are a modified stem, and as they spread out and fill the pot, new fronds occur at various points, seeming to materialize from the soil.

The stalks that bear the fronds are rather stiff, and stand upright more than most ferns do. This is another reason these plants do well on a table—the tips don't so easily bang into the furniture.

Humidity   All ferns like humid atmosphere; give this one a misting, or keep it on a pebble tray. Because of its upright shape, this fern is easier to keep

Pteris cretica

on a pebble tray than those you would rather put in a hanging basket.

Water   In spring and summer, water when soil feels dry; give less water in winter.

Temperature   Normal house temperature, as long as it isn't *too* hot.

Light   Ideal position is a north window—in other words, not much direct sun. Will tolerate poor light conditions and artificial light.

Propagation   Division.

Rhapis excelsa   Lady palm
RAY-pis ex-SELL-sah   Little lady palm
                                Bamboo palm

If you have ever traveled or lived where palms grow outdoors, chances are you have a special feeling for these marvelous trees. They seem to capture, in flora, the very essence of the tropics. And you will really enjoy having them as houseplants, for unlike some houseplants that are baby trees but bear little resemblance to the outdoor specimens, indoor palms really do have much of the same character and personality as their outdoor brethren. And guess what? They are easy to grow.

The lady palm, from southern China, is a charmer. It gets tall enough to notice, but not so huge that you have to worry about it hitting your ceiling. Its leaves (called fronds in palms) are composed of long, thin leaflets that spread out in a circle from a central point. There are about half a dozen leaflets per frond, and often they are blunt on the ends, as if trimmed off with scissors.

The trunk looks somewhat like a bamboo cane, and the fronds grow out all around it. Often several palms are planted together in one pot, creating a bushy look. Lady palm grows slowly indoors, but will eventually reach a height of about five feet.

Caring for this graceful palm is not difficult. It will forgive you if your watering habits are less than perfect, and it doesn't need high humidity. It doesn't need a lot of light either, and in fact will burn up in direct sun.

The one thing it does need that may take some planning on your part is cool temperatures. If you have a room that you don't heat as much in the wintertime as the rest of the house, that's a good place. Another good spot might be an entryway; this plant can stand the drafts.

Humidity   Not something you have to worry about.

Water   Keep the soil lightly moist (and be sure it drains well).

Rhapis excelsa

230

Temperature Cool; under 65 degrees if possible.

Light Will survive quite low light, but prefers semishade.

Propagation Not really practical for homes.

Saintpaulia
saint-PAUL-ee-ah   African violet

In the forests of the Usambara Mountains in eastern Africa, located in what is now Tanzania, there grow several species of a small flowering plant with fuzzy leaves and violetlike flowers.

Before World War I, that area was part of the territory known as German East Africa, owned by Germany and administered by men who came to Africa from Germany to help run the government of the colony. Baron Walter von Saint Paul, one such colonial official, was a man who enjoyed nature and gardening. On one of his walks in the mountains he came across this small flower, which he had not seen before, and decided to send a few plants to his father back in Germany.

The elder von Saint Paul, so the story goes, took the plants to the head of the Royal Botanical Garden for examination. That gentleman realized it was a species unknown in Europe, and named the ''new'' plant *Saintpaulia* in honor of the men who had brought it to his attention.

After breeding and studying the new plant for a few years, the botanist realized that there were actually two different species. One he named *Saintpaulia ionantha* (meaning ''like a violet'') and the other was called *Saintpaulia confusa,* thus immortalizing the original confusion.

From those two species literally thousands of African violet hybrids have been developed, since the first samples were sent to Germany a hundred years ago. And new ones are being developed every day.

There are African violets with plain leaves, ruffled leaves, curled leaves, and straight leaves, all-green leaves and leaves edged with white. The flowers may be white, pink, mauve, purple, blue, lavender, red, or a combination of colors. The flowers may have a single layer of petals, or double; the petals may be smooth or ruffled. There are standard-size plants, miniatures, and trailing varieties.

African violets have an enormous following of enthusiastic growers; whole books are devoted to their culture. There is a

Saintpaulia ionantha

national African Violet Society, with chapters in most medium or large cities; the society publishes a bimonthly magazine. You will find the plants for sale everywhere—in supermarkets and variety stores, as well as the more traditional sources of houseplants. Most people who buy one, soon buy others.

All this should help dispel the common belief that African violets are difficult to grow. You can't completely turn your back on them, as you can a cactus, but they are not the cantankerous devils they are made out to be. The new hybrids are bred for sturdiness.

We grow African violets for the flowers, and the most important factor for blooming is the proper light. An ideal location is a south or west window that is shaded by a deciduous tree; in winter, when the sun is lower, the leaves will be off the tree and the plant will get the light it needs. If your south window has no tree to diffuse the bright summer sun, make sure it has a sheer curtain.

African violets also respond very well indeed to artificial light, and many people successfully grow them in rooms with very poor natural light by adding a fluorescent fixture (regular incandescent light bulbs don't have the right kind of light, and anyway they get too hot for the plant). With this artificial light supplementing natural light, you can have flowers all year round.

Green Thumb Tip

If you're an African violet beginner, keep these two points in mind:

1. Plants with plain leaves are hardier than plants with ruffled leaves.

2. If your light is less than perfect, choose plants with plain, not variegated, leaves; choose plants whose leaves are pale green on top and silvery underneath, rather than dark green on top and red below.

The best setup is a fixture that has room for two bulbs; get one that has mostly the blue end of the color spectrum (usually labeled "cool white") and one that has the red end (called "warm white" or "daylight"). Or you can buy fluorescent lights made especially for houseplants, called "grow lights." In any case, don't leave the lights on all the time; the plants need a normal period of darkness.

In addition to light, the other concern is proper watering. With African violets, as with many other indoor plants, less is better than more. Water only when the top of the soil is dry. Don't let the runoff stay in the saucer. Don't use cold water or water with fluorine in it; if your municipal water supply is fluoridated, fill your watering can and let it sit overnight. And *don't* pour the water onto the leaves or the center of the plant.

The stems of the leaves are very soft and juicy, and rot easily. The same is true of the roots, which is why you don't want the pot to sit in water. For the same reason, the soil must be very porous, so that water drains easily. In plant stores you will find a special potting mix just for African violets; many experts use this and still add an equal measure of perlite or vermiculite.

These plants like humidity and do nicely on a pebble tray. (Don't spray them, for water drops can spot the leaves.) Many people have them on windowsills, which is fine as long as the area doesn't get very cold at night.

Some people who grow lots of African violets feel that it's not a good idea for the leaves to touch the edges of the pot. To protect the soft leaves, they cover the rim with aluminum foil, or paint a thin coat of melted paraffin on the rim.

One of the joys of African violets is growing your own plants from a leaf and sharing with a friend. To start a new plant, follow these steps.

1. Choose a healthy and mature leaf, not a young one; one that is halfway up from the outermost ring of leaves would be about right.
2. With a sharp knife or razor blade, cut off the leaf and all of its stem. You can also pull it off with a sideways motion if you are careful.

3. Trim off the leaf stem down to one inch, using a slanted cut.
4. Set the leaf aside for an hour, to let the cut end dry.
5. Meanwhile, prepare the rooting container—a small pot, or even a paper cup (punch a drainage hole in the bottom)— with a damp mixture of vermiculite, perlite, and sand. (You can also use water; see no. 11 below.)
6. With a pencil or chopstick, make a slanting hole in the pot and insert the leaf stem, so that the leaf is lying gently against the edge of the pot.
7. If you're doing more than one, write the variety name on a piece of masking tape and tape it to the leaf.
8. Cover lightly with a plastic bag, to retain moisture; check periodically to see that the rooting medium hasn't dried out. Careful, though: not too wet, or the leaf will rot.

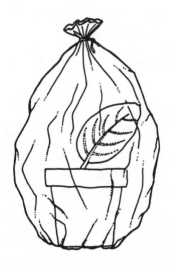

One healthy leaf from an African violet plant can be used to start a new plant. Cover with plastic bag to create a greenhouse effect and speed up the rooting process.

9. In a few weeks you will see tiny plants starting to grow at the base of the leaf. Cut off half the original leaf so it doesn't block the light from the babies.

When a young plant starts to develop, remove the plastic bag. You may want to trim off part of the "parent" leaf, so the baby gets more light.

10. When the baby plants have leaves the size of a nickel, they can be lifted out and transplanted to their own pots. Or, if you have just one cutting rooting in a small pot, cut away the parent leaf and leave the baby to develop in the pot.

When the baby plant is fully formed, remove from water jar or soil. Cut away and discard the original leaf, and move the new plant to its own pot.

11. To root a leaf cutting in water, fill a container with water and add a few small pieces of charcoal. Cover the container with aluminum or plastic, and punch holes with a pencil. Roots and a baby plant will form underwater.

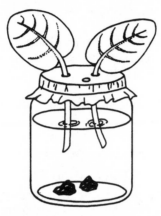

Leaf cuttings of African violets can be rooted in water as well as soil. To keep the leaves from falling out of the jar, cover container with aluminum foil, plastic wrap, or waxed paper, and punch holes just big enough for the stems. A few pieces of charcoal will keep the water "sweet," but this is optional. A new plant, with roots, will form at the base of the stem, underwater.

The plant also reproduces itself by producing small offset plants (called suckers). They appear at the base of the plant, or sometimes down between the leaves. To preserve the vigor of the original plant, these suckers should be removed. If you lift them out carefully, you can move them to their own pot and have new plants.

And finally, to keep the flowers coming, you need to fertilize your violets. There are plant fertilizers formulated especially for African violets, and these are probably the easiest to use. Many people have best success by fertilizing with a very thinly diluted mixture (one-quarter strength or less) every time they water.

Humidity	Higher than average house humidity. Keep on a pebble tray.
Water	Let soil get dry on top before watering.
Temperature	Normal house, but not below 60 degrees.
Light	Needs bright light (but not direct sun) in order to produce flower buds. Responds very well to artificial lighting.
Propagation	Leaf cuttings. Remove and pot offsets.

Decorating Tip

African violets, with their rounded shape, look very beautiful in a circular glass bowl; this holds in humidity and shows off the blossoms. But planting it terrarium style runs the risk of waterlogging the roots. Solution: Keep the plant in its pot, set it into the bowl, on a few pebbles; if you wish, fill in all around with peat moss to disguise the pot. Make sure the bowl has an opening large enough for you to get in and snip off dead flowers.

Another nice display technique is to group several pots together into a shallow basket; this way the plants help humidify each other.

Thanks to the Portland, Oregon, African Violet Society for sharing tips on keeping these beautiful plants. To learn more, contact the African Violet Society of America, P.O. Box 3609, Beaumont, Texas 77704. Membership is $15 a year, and includes a subscription to the society's magazine, published six times a year.

Sansevieria trifasciata
san-sev-ee-AIRY-ah
try-fass-ee-AH-tah

Snake plant
Mother-in-law's tongue
Bowstring hemp
Devil's tongue

There are a few plants that will grow for anyone anywhere under any circumstances—and this is one.

It's a desert plant from arid Africa, a succulent that stores water in its very thick, tough leaves. So you don't have to be around to water it every few days. In addition, it's an exception to the rule that succulents need sun; this plant will grow in any dark corner you put it in. It can stay in the same pot for years. It doesn't need extra humidity; in fact it prefers dry air. So you don't have to do anything at all to keep it alive, except restrain yourself from giving it too much water. This plant will survive the severest neglect.

What you get in return for all this neglect may or may not be called beautiful—that's for you to say—but it is something green that will grow where nothing else will. This is a tall, upright plant, with a completely vertical growth pattern. The plant is all leaf; each tall, spiky leaf comes up from underground without any real stem. The leaves twist ever so slightly, giving them the look of underwater plants moving with the currents.

The leaves are about an inch wide and usually about three feet tall; they are dark green, with horizontal bands of gray-green. This coloring, in combination with the long narrow shape, makes the leaf look like a snake.

A mature plant grows by sending out short underground stems, from which a new plant sprouts an inch or so away. This offshoot plant can be cut from the parent (use a very sharp knife) and started in a new pot. Or you can leave it where it is, and eventually your original pot will be filled with tall, graceful spears of green. You can also make leaf cuttings to propagate new plants; you'll get several from one leaf. Follow these steps:

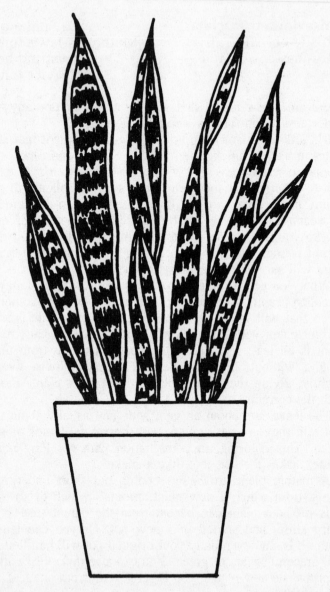

Sansevieria trifasciata 'Laurentii'

1. Cut off one healthy leaf with a sharp knife.
2. Cut it into three-inch segments.
3. With a felt-tip marker, mark the top of each segment.

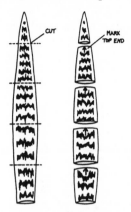

To propagate snake plant, cut one leaf away from the plant, down at the soil line. Then, with a sharp knife, cut that leaf into segments. Keep them lined up until you have clearly marked which end of each segment is the top; you can use a felt-tip pen.

4. Let the pieces dry for a few days until the cut ends are no longer sticky.
5. Plant the "bottom" end about one inch deep in moist sand or vermiculite.

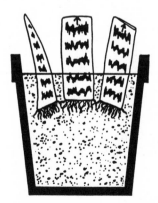

After the cut ends have dried, plant the segments in damp sand. Make sure the bottom end is down and the top end is up, otherwise nothing will happen.

6. Keep the sand damp, and be patient.
7. The cutting will send out a short stem and a new plant will sprout; the original stem piece will wither.
8. When it's about an inch tall, you can move the new plant (discard any remains of the cutting) into its own pot.

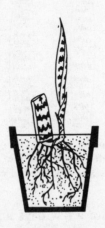

After several weeks, a new plant will form off to the side. If you have several segments rooting in one pot, move each to its own pot. If you have just one, cut away the original segment and leave the infant to develop right in that pot.

Other Varieties

Sansevieria trifasciata 'Laurentii' is just like the basic species except it also has a stripe of creamy yellow running down both edges.

Sansevieria trifasciata 'Hahnii'

S. t. 'Hahnii' is a low-growing rosette shape, very attractive.

S. t. 'Golden Hahnii' has the same low rosette shape with the addition of golden yellow stripes on the edges.

Humidity   Dry air is not a problem.

Water   Like a cactus: let soil go dry, water deeply, don't water again until it's really dry.

Temperature Tolerates a very wide range.

Light   Will take whatever it can get; one of the rare succulents that will grow in dim corners.

Propagation Offsets. Leaf cuttings.

Schefflera actinophylla   Umbrella plant
sheff-LEER-ah act-tin-OFF-i-lah   Octopus tree
                             Queensland umbrella tree

The elegant schefflera is popular with people who want a big, tree-size plant. In time it will easily reach seven or eight feet; in its home environment in Australia, it gets to be fifty feet tall.

Much of its appeal as a houseplant comes from the unusual leaves. A leaf is composed of a number of leaflets, all set in a circle around a central stem and stretching out horizontally, like the ribs of an umbrella. Each leaflet is a pointy oval, six to eight inches long, and a rich shiny green.

As it gets older, schefflera loses leaves from the lower part of the stem, increasing its tree shape.

The broad leaves tend to collect dust, and this in turn seems to be attractive to red spider mites. To help keep them under control, and to keep your plant looking its best, keep the leaves dusted.

This plant will accommodate itself to your environment reasonably well. It will accept normal household temperatures, and adapts to our humidity (although it would prefer more). As long as you can give it reasonably good light, and keep it clean, you should have it around to enjoy for a long time.

Humidity   Give it a spray from your misting bottle when you think of it.

Water   Spring and summer, keep soil lightly damp; fall and winter, water when soil is dry an inch down.

Temperature Tolerates a wide range. Enjoys the fresh outdoor air in summer.

Light   Bright filtered light is ideal; a semisunny location is also good. Do not put in direct sun.

Schefflera

Propagation	Cut off and transplant the offsets that sprout at the base of the plant.
Problems	Susceptible to red spider mites; keep the plant free of dust.

Schlumbergera
shlum-BUR-ger-ah

Christmas cactus
Thanksgiving cactus

A jungle cactus with leaves linked one after the other like a chain, ending in a blast of glorious flowers that bloom in winter at holiday time. The flowers are truly sensational, and they are the whole reason for having these plants; in nonflowering times, the plant is boring.

But is it a Christmas cactus or a Thanksgiving cactus? For a long time, two different genus names were used.

Zygocactus truncatus was called Thanksgiving cactus because it blooms closer to Thanksgiving. Its leaf segments have sharply jagged ends.

Schlumbergera bridgesii was called Christmas cactus because it blooms a little later; its leaf segments have scalloped ends with no sharp points.

Today, all the species and the many varieties are put into just one genus: *Schlumbergera*. However, in plant stores you will still see the name *Zygocactus* used. To make matters worse, the blooming time can be manipulated in greenhouses, so we can't depend on the calendar to tell us which plant we're looking at. By controlling the amount of light and water a plant receives, growers can force it to bloom in sync with the holiday retail season.

The only positive way to tell the difference is the look of the leaves. *Schlumbergera truncatus* (trun-CAY-tus) is the one with the sharp points at the ends of the leaf segments; the common name of "crab cactus" is a good clue. The leaf segments of *Schlumbergera bridgesii* (bridge-EASY-eye) have rounded, scalloped ends.

As a practical matter, however, there really isn't a great deal of difference. Because of the many varieties that have been developed, both species are available in a range of wonderful

Schlumbergera

colors—pink, red, deep rose, lavender, orange, and recently yellow. And both can be manipulated to bloom at certain times (within a range of the plant's natural proclivities, that is).

Generally you find these for sale a few weeks ahead of the holiday season. Most will have some blooms already open, so you can tell what color flowers it will have. Choose one that has lots of unopened flower buds, and you'll have flowers to enjoy for several weeks to come.

When you first bring your plant home, put it in a spot that gets bright light but is rather cool—a bedroom, perhaps. The sudden change from greenhouse to your house can cause flower buds to drop off all at once. Using a cool spot for a few days will make the transition much easier.

After all the flowers fade, the plant needs a rest period. If you live in the Sun Belt, you can set the pot outdoors; choose a spot where it gets some protection from direct rays of the sun. If it freezes in early spring in your part of the country, keep the plant indoors until it warms up outside. In either case, water lightly and fertilize regularly.

To help your plant bloom again the next year, follow these steps:

1. Mid-September, bring the plant inside (if it has been outdoors). Put it in a room that is cool at night (55 to 60 degrees).
2. Give the plant much less water. Wait till the leaves start to get limp before watering.
3. Make sure the plant is in darkness at least twelve hours a day. That means put it in a room you don't use in the evening (even a closet), or cover it with a black plastic bag till morning. This is what florists call "short-day treatment."
4. In three or four weeks, you will see tiny flower buds forming. At that point you can put the plant wherever you want, and resume normal watering.

On the other hand, you will hear people say with great conviction that they don't do any of this; they just keep the plant in the same place all year long, and it blooms year after year. Some of these folks have plants that are twenty or thirty years old, so who can argue with them? You may get good results with this more casual approach, but the short-day treatment increases your chances for success.

The flowers are at the very end of the last leaf, which means that a very mature plant, with leaf stalks three or four feet long, will have all its blossoms clustered down at the end. If you want a mass of flowers all around the plant, prune some of the stems. To do this, twist a segment right at the joint and it should snap off easily.

You can now root the pruned-off segments in damp sand, and start new plants. How about a baby Christmas cactus for next year's Christmas presents?

This cactus is not a desert plant. It comes from the jungles of eastern Brazil, where it grows hanging on trees.

Humidity	While this plant is indoors, extra humidity would be appreciated.
Water	When the soil is dry an inch down, water. During the time flower buds are forming, and after flowering is over, water less.
Temperature	Cool nights are needed for flower buds to form; otherwise, normal house temperature will do.
Light	Bright filtered light will keep flowers coming on. Needs twelve hours of complete darkness nightly for about a month for flower buds to develop.
Propagation	Leaf segments root easily. Let a segment dry for a day or so, till the end is no longer wet, then insert in damp sand, bottom side down.

Sedum morganianum   Burro tail
SEE-dum mor-gan-ee-AH-num   Donkey tail

The *Sedum* genus has about five hundred different species, found all over the world, and there is an enormously wide range in their size, leaf shape, and growth pattern. Many are rounded, ground-hugging plants featured in outdoor rock gardens. In ancient days the Romans grew them on the roofs of houses, where the roots held them in place.

The species that are used as indoor plants come mostly from the dry regions of Mexico. Burro tail is one of the more popular and widely available species, and is presented here as typical of what all sedums need in terms of care.

Burro tail has tiny leaves, about half an inch long, that are very tightly packed along the stem. At the base, where they join the stem, they overlap like roof shingles. The leaves are gray-green, very fat, and have a waxy surface that helps keep water from being lost through the leaves.

The stems trail down as they get longer and will eventually reach perhaps three feet. Because the little leaves are rather easily knocked off, the best way to grow this plant is in a hanging basket away from traffic.

As the plant gets older, the oldest leaves, those near the center of the plant, shrivel up and fall off, leaving ugly bare stems. Unfortunately, new leaves won't grow to replace them—all new growth is at the outer end of the stem—and so the bare stems remain bare unless you step in. The remedy seems severe, but it's the only way: cut the stems back beyond the section that is bare, and wait for new leaves to grow at the cut point.

While you're waiting, you can root the sections you cut off. If they are long (and often they are), divide them into pieces about three inches long and stand them in moist sand. When they're rooted, put them back in your original pot, and start the process all over. It's also possible to root individual leaves, but then what you have is a very, very small plant.

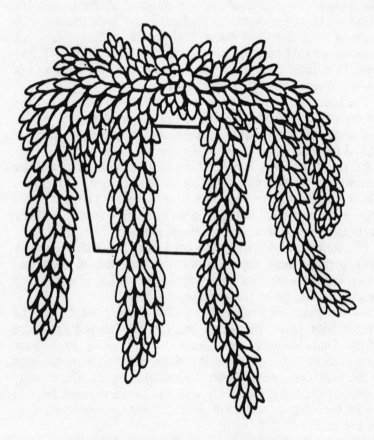

Sedum morganianum

Sedums are succulents, desert plants. Their leaves and stems are especially designed to store water for long periods, so they don't need lots of water from you. Make sure the soil mix is one that drains well; you may need to add sand. Being desert plants, they also love sun.

Humidity   You don't have to worry about humidity with sedums; they like dry air.

Water   Treat them like cactus: let soil go almost completely dry before watering.

Temperature   Normal house temperature is fine.

Light   Bright sunlight.

Propagation   Stem cuttings root in damp sand. Sometimes the leaves that naturally fall off will take root in the soil they land on.

Setcreasea purpurea
set-CREASE-ee-ah purr-poo-REE-ah

Purple heart
Wandering jew

This is one of several kinds of plants that are called wandering jew. They all grow the same way, and all need essentially the same kind of care. The outstanding trait of this particular one is its wonderful color: it is a rich regal purple all over.

There is one other difference as well: the leaves of purple heart are quite a bit larger than most other wandering jews: three or four inches long. They are covered all over with very fine hairs, giving the plant a somewhat velvety look.

Purple heart has a lanky, sprawly way of growing, and can easily get to be messy looking. Keep it pinched faithfully, and if it gets out of control, take lots of cuttings and start off with a new plant in the spring. Cuttings root very easily at any node (that slightly thick part of the stem where a leaf is attached). In the wild, this plant grows along the ground and roots wherever a node touches soil.

To keep the color bright, this plant needs to be in good light. In sunlight, it may even bloom: a tiny pink flower appears at the end of the stem.

Purple heart is a native of Mexico and was introduced as a houseplant in the mid-1950s—relatively recent, as houseplants go.

Humidity	Average house humidity is fine.
Water	Water moderately in summer; in winter, let soil get dry one inch down before watering.
Temperature	Indoor temperatures are fine.
Light	Bright sunshine will keep the color; in dimmer light, the leaves slowly become green.
Propagation	Stem cuttings root extremely easily.

Setcreasea purpurea

Problems   Leggy growth. Get in the habit of pinching. Start lots of cuttings, and be ready to discard plant when it gets too untidy.

Spathiphyllum   Peace lily
spath-ee-FILE-um   White flag
                                                     White sails
                                                     Spath flower

There are some people who don't feel they're doing right by
their plants unless they're *doing* something to them, and the
thing they most like to do is water them. If you're one of
them, here's the plant for you.

Spaths (to use their best nickname) like their soil evenly
moist at all times. Depending on the temperature in your living
room, you may need to water every three or four days. Actually, the plant itself will tell you when it's thirsty—the
leaves suddenly get droopy and collapse like a deflated bal-
loon. Give it a good drink, until water runs out the drainage
holes, and it recovers almost immediately, with no harm done.
It's so satisfying to watch this recovery, it's sometimes tempting to deliberately underwater, but that's not recommended.

This plant is an all-around winner. It produces very striking
flowers in areas where few other indoor plants will bloom; the
lush foliage is very handsome; you can grow it successfully
in low light; and it's easy to care for. One testimony to its
toughness: it's very popular in shopping-mall planters.

The flower is very prominent and very showy—white
against the dark green of the leaves. It looks a bit like a lily,
even more like a Jack-in-the-pulpit. Actually, the true flower
is the yellow spike inside the white cup (the white petal is
technically called a spathe), but most people just call the whole
thing the flower.

The flower sits at the end of a long thin stem, which pro-
trudes up above the leaves; each flower will live for a long
time, as much as a month. When the flower yellows and dies,
trim off the entire stalk.

Even when it is not flowering, the spath is an extremely
handsome plant. Overall, the plant can be two to three feet
tall, with very full and lush foliage. Its leaves are a dark,

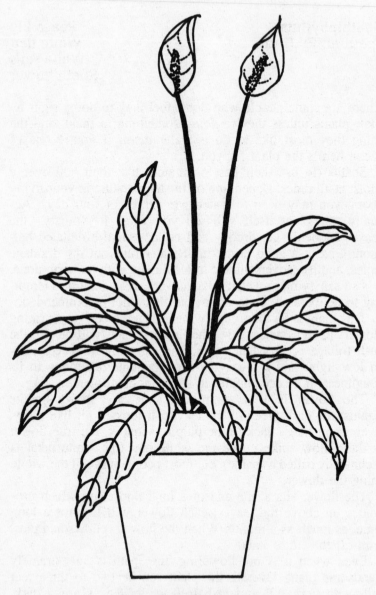

Spathiphyllum

lustrous green, long ovals on stems that come up directly from the soil and arch gracefully. Leaves are six to twelve inches long, depending on the species (see below), and two to four inches wide, with a very prominent point at the tip.

Spathiphyllum grows naturally in the tropical areas of Central and South America, and would be happiest in a similar environment indoors—high humidity, damp soil, partial sunshine. Luckily for us, however, this is a tough plant and will adjust to less than ideal conditions. One of its strongest features is that it will survive in low-light areas.

This plant is a vigorous grower and will probably need repotting every year. While you're doing that, you might want to divide the clumps and pot them individually. A grouping of several pots of spaths massed together is very attractive.

Varieties

Spathiphyllum clevelandii has leaves ten or twelve inches long, and its flower is about four inches.

S. wallisii is much the same but smaller.

S. floribunda has small leaves but almost constant flowers ("floribunda" means "many flowers").

Humidity	Prefers high humidity and will be grateful for regular misting (or keep small plants on a pebble tray), but will adapt to normal house humidity.
Water	Keep the soil damp.
Temperature	Average house temperatures are fine.
Light	Ideally, bright filtered light; will survive in less but with fewer flowers.
Propagation	Division.

SUCCULENTS

The word "succulent" occurs often in books about houseplants, and it can be a bit confusing. When it is used as a noun, "succulent" means any of a large group of plants that have developed ways of storing water—in their leaves, stems, or roots, or all three—to survive the dry climates where they grow naturally. There are several families, many genera, and many, many species.

In this sense of the word, a cactus is a succulent. But because cacti are so specialized, we think of them as a completely separate group. All cacti are succulents, but not all succulents are cacti. Not by a long shot.

The word is also used as an adjective: we speak of "succulent leaves" or "semisucculent stems" or "succulent root structures." This is a more generalized usage, and simply means that the part of the plant hold moisture in their tissues more than most plants do. In other words, it is possible to describe as "succulent" part of a plant that is technically not a succulent. Wandering jew, for instance, has soft, very watery stems; we could say they are "succulent," even though wandering jew is not *a* succulent.

It's tricky to describe all succulents as a group, for there are some surprising exceptions; some you would swear, just by appearance, are not succulents at all. Speaking very generally, though, succulents have thick, firm leaves and often thick stems as well. Their leaves are smooth and rather waxy on the surface; this is the plant's way of storing moisture. All plants lose water vapor through their leaves; it is part of their cycle of respiration. But those with waxy leaves lose it at a slower rate.

By and large, succulents grow in arid regions with poor soil. They are slow growers. As indoor plants, they don't mind dry air, they don't want a lot of water, and they don't need repotting often, all of which makes them easy to care for. They also need lots of sun, which makes them problematic for some homes.

In this book you will find descriptions and illustrations of the following succulents:

Ceropegia woodii *Kalanchoe*
Crassula argentea *Sansevieria*
Echeveria elegans *Sedum morganianum*

These are among the most popular, but there are many, many others, with a very wide range of shapes and sizes. You may come across:

- *Agave,* known as "century plant." Outdoor species are enormous, with towering flower stalks.
- *Aloe,* including *Aloe vera,* which is added to over-the-counter burn medications; if you cut off a piece of leaf and rub the cut end on a burn, it works the same way.
- *Euphorbia,* a genus that includes—believe it or not—poinsettia.
- *Lithops,* called "living stones," "stoneface," or "stoneplant" because they really do look exactly like pebbles.
- *Sempervivum* species, which usually have small leaves growing in a tight rosette; young plants, called offsets, are tightly clustered around the mother (several species are known as "hen and chickens"). When they reach a certain age, the offsets themselves produce offsets. The plant thus perpetually reproduces itself; *sempervivum* means "lives forever."

- *Senecio* includes a plant called "string of beads." Its small, completely round leaves are attached to long threadlike stems that dangle attractively when the plant is grown in a hanging container.

Syngonium podophyllum
sin-GOH-nee-um pod-oh-FILE-um

Arrowhead vine
Goosefoot plant
African evergreen
Trileaf wonder

This vine comes from the tropical rain forests of Central America—just like that all-time favorite, the philodendron; indeed, it looks and grows a lot like the philodendron, and takes pretty much the same kind of care.

As a young plant, syngonium grows upright, its arrow-shaped leaves at the end of a short stem. With time, it becomes apparent that this is really a vine, for the new growth starts creeping downward (if your plant is in a hanging basket) or climbing upward (if it has a pole or stake to grab on to). You can also keep it relatively small and bushy if you prefer: pinch out the growing tip, and the plant will branch out sideways.

The characteristic of this plant that creates the most interest is the varied shape of the leaves. When the plant is very young, all the leaves are shaped like a triangle with a deep notch at the base, where the stem is attached; the common name of "arrowhead vine" describes it best. As it gets older, the plant produces leaves with deep scallops, sort of like a starfish. One plant will often have several kinds of leaves at the same time.

There are several different species and varieties available; the main difference is the leaves, which may be variegated with yellow or white. In nurseries and shops, this plant is often labeled "Nephthytis" (NEFF-the-tiss).

Like its philodendron relatives, this is an easy plant; with just minimal attention from you, it will thrive indoors. Cuttings root very easily and will live for a long time in water.

Humidity   Likes humid air but will adapt to normal house humidity levels. Appreciates misting now and then.

Water   Keep very lightly damp in summer, drier in winter. Overwatering is a common mistake.

Syngonium

Temperature   Normal house; keep out of drafts.

Light   Tolerates a wide range, from bright filtered to shady corners; don't put in direct full sun.

Propagation   Stem cuttings root easily, especially sections with aerial roots already showing.

Tolmiea menziesii   Piggyback plant
TOLE-mee-ah men-ZEE-   Mother of thousands
zee-eye   Youth on age

Most of the species that we know as houseplants grow wild in exotic parts of the world: the Polynesian islands, the jungles of South America, the deserts of Mexico and South Africa. This one grows in our backyard—that is, if you happen to live on the West Coast. This plant is native to the forests of the coast ranges from California to Alaska.

Indoors it's a rather small plant, with a soft, rounded shape and a bright green color. The leaves are essentially heart-shaped with lightly jagged edges, and covered all over with fine hairs that give the plant a soft, furry texture.

But the principal charm of this plant is the method by which it reproduces itself. At the point where the leaf joins its stem, a small baby plant is produced; it sits on top of a short stalk, and thus seems to ride piggyback on top of the parent leaf. It's very entertaining.

Making new plants is a snap. Trim off a leaf that is carrying a baby, set it in damp soil so the baby is aboveground, and before long it will set roots. Then cut the rooted baby away from the parent leaf and transplant it to its own pot. If your original plant has grown stems that extend outward far enough, you can just set a mother leaf, still attached to the plant, in a small nearby pot and cut it off when rooted; this method is a bit faster.

The piggyback plant likes conditions that mimic its forest homeland: humid air, coolish temperatures, damp soil, semi-shaded light.

A word of caution: this is not the easiest plant to keep healthy year after year. It is prone to both red spider mites and mealybugs, and because of the way the plant grows, with overlapping leaves, both are difficult to eradicate. Commonsense guideline: if your plant gets infected, discard it and buy another.

Tolmiea menziesii

Humidity	Does best in humidity that is higher than most houses (although it will adapt). Don't spray it; you'll spot the foliage. Set it on a pebble tray.
Water	Lightly damp.
Temperature	On the cool side: 60 to 65 degrees in the daytime, to 55 at night.
Light	Will accept semishady conditions.
Propagation	Leaf cutting, when baby plant is present.
Problems	Susceptible to red spider and mealybugs; a cool, humid location will help to control.
Special features	Children are enchanted with the baby plants taking a piggyback ride on their mother's back. Give children a leaf to root for their own.

Tradescantia
tray-dess-CAN-tee-ah

Wandering jew
Giant inch plant
Speedy Jenny
Chain plant

King Charles I of England had two men named John Tradescant—father and son—serving as royal gardeners. Both were dedicated scientists who traveled extensively, collecting plant specimens and bringing them back to England for study and experimentation; the elder Tradescant brought many species from as far away as Russia, and his son sailed to Virginia in the New World in search of new specimens.

The trailing, creeping vine in the genus *Tradescantia* was probably not discovered by them, for it's a native of Central and South America, but it was named in honor of these two horticultural pioneers of the seventeenth century.

This plant gets its common names from the way it grows. The stems are jointed at regular distances (in some species, the joints are an inch apart), rather like a chain, and it "wanders" all over its terrain, branching and spreading in all directions. Wherever a stem joint touches soil, roots form.

In very warm climates, wandering jew is grown outdoors as a ground cover. Indoors, it is usually grown in a hanging basket, and can trail down to a length of several feet. It is a tough plant, easy to grow and hard to kill. Your main chore will be keeping it nicely shaped, for it is a vigorous grower and will get leggy quickly.

To prevent this, keep pinching it back. This will encourage the stems to branch out sideways, producing a fuller look. And then you can put the part you cut off in a glass of water, where it will root in the blink of an eye.

You may find that some of your stems are nice and full at the outer end but empty and leggy near the base. If you just can't stand the thought of cutting off the healthy part, you can loop the end back over the soil and pin it down (use something like an old-fashioned hairpin), and it will take root there.

Tradescantia

But this is really a second-best approach. A cutting of wandering jew roots so quickly, so easily, that this is a good plant for you to practice on. Go ahead and cut that scraggly stem way back at the soil line; watch how quickly the cut end sends out new growth. The cuttings that you are rooting in water will live in water for a long time.

When you take a cutting, notice how watery and juicy the stems are. That is the sign of a semisucculent plant, and that is your signal to take it easy on the watering. The best approach is, wait till the soil is dry about an inch down, then really soak it, then let dry out before watering again.

There are several species of *Tradescantia* and many varieties, offering houseplant enthusiasts a nice range of colorful leaves: bright green, pale green, green-and-silver striped, some tinged with soft pink, some with magenta undersides. The brighter the coloring, the more sun the plant needs.

(Wandering jew is the common name of several genera; see also *Setcreasea purpurea* and *Zebrina pendula*.)

Humidity	Normal house humidity is fine.
Water	Very lightly moist; let soil go dry on top before watering.
Temperature	Not fussy about temperature.
Light	Varieties with intense coloring and variegation need bright but filtered light; plants with green leaves can take dimmer areas.
Propagation	Stem cuttings root in a jiffy.

Zebrina pendula
zuh-BREE-nah pen-DEW-lah

Wandering jew
Wandering sailor
Zebra plant

The genus *Zebrina* is named for the Latin word that means striped, and the leaves have colorful striping running down lengthwise. The leaves are attached to the stems at joints about an inch apart, and the trailing stems grow profusely in a hanging basket.

Doesn't that sound like a description of the genus *Tradescantia*? In fact, the two are often confused. It is very difficult for someone who's not a trained botanist to tell the difference between a *Tradescantia* and a *Zebrina*. They have a very similar look, similar growing habit, and the same common name: wandering jew.

As a very general rule of thumb, a pale green-and-white striped leaf is probably *Tradescantia*. A plant with leaves that are purple on the bottom and green-and-white striped on top is probably *Zebrina*. As a practical matter, it isn't really significant, since both need pretty much the same care.

This wandering jew will grow leggy and lanky if not in good light, and will need a haircut regularly. Don't be bashful—new leaves will grow quickly from the cut end, and the parts you cut off will root *very* quickly in a glass of water. If you don't keep trimming the growing end, you'll end up with a mess: beautiful leaves down at the bottom of scraggly bare stems.

Humidity   Will adapt to normal house humidity.

Water   On the dry side: let top layer of soil go dry before you water.

Temperature   Average house.

Zebrina

Light	To maintain the brilliant leaf color, keep in bright filtered light. Will grow in lower light, but color will fade.
Propagation	Stem cuttings root very easily.

4

🍒 🍒 🍒

Nurturing Your Houseplants:
Basic Day-to-Day Care

Taking care of houseplants involves two groups of activities: things you have to do only once in a while, and things you have to do on a regular basis. This chapter will explain the day-to-day, week-to-week basics:

- Watering
- Light
- Humidity
- Fertilizing
- Pruning
- Grooming

When you buy plants at the store, often they come with little white plastic sticks giving instructions on how to care for them. A friendly word of caution: Take those instructions with a large dose of salt. They are too skimpy to be really useful; sometimes they are inaccurate; and sometimes the wrong stick got put in the pot. You're much better off taking an extra minute or two to look up your new plant and read about its care needs.

Watering

For overall good health, two things are absolutely critical to indoor plants: light and water. Both are important, but watering is the part that seems to cause the most confusion, and without doubt it causes the most problems, so we'll discuss it first.

Too Much, Too Little
Why do plants need water?

1. To keep the cells plump and healthy, so the plant stands up instead of sagging.
2. To be able to pull water-soluble minerals out of the soil.

These minerals are a necessary part of photosynthesis, the chemical process by which the plant manufactures its food. The only way the plant can get them is to draw them up through the roots after they become dissolved in water. So even if the lack of water didn't affect the leaves, the plant would soon die for lack of nutrition. We should be grateful that the leaves do droop, for that calls our attention to the problem, usually in time to remedy it.

So having no water for a long time is a problem. But having too much water, which is far more common, is a far bigger problem. Here's why: in the pot, normally the tiny spaces between the particles of soil are filled with air, and so the tiny root hairs reaching all around are in contact with oxygen, which is necessary if photosynthesis is going to take place. But when you oversaturate the soil with water, so that the pot is waterlogged, those tiny spaces are completely filled with water, driving the air out.

The plant is surrounded by water but is physically unable to take any water in, and so it reacts just the same as if it had no water at all: it droops and withers and the leaves turn yellow. It appears that it lacks water, so in a frantic effort to save it, you pour on even more water. The next thing you know, you have the problem of root rot; the roots, festering in this waterlogged soil, will literally rot. It's the same as having no roots at all, and the plant will die.

More damage is done to plants by too much water than by too little—by a long shot. They will usually recover from underwatering, but overwatering is often fatal.

The Right Amount

So how much water does a plant need? It would be nice if we could follow a set rule—two cups of water every Friday—but things just don't work that way. Remember that the plants are very different from one another; some come from a desert environment, some from a humid jungle, some from a cool rain forest. The amount of water that is right varies from one plant to the next. You have to learn the water needs of each of your plants.

Unfortunately, even for a specific plant, it isn't possible to describe watering in terms of volume. We can't say "a quart, a cup" because the right amount of water for any particular plant depends on many factors; to make matters worse, those factors change.

- A plant needs more water in the spring and summer, when it is actively growing, than in the winter, when it is resting.
- A plant needs more water in a warm room than in a cool room.
- A plant in a plastic pot needs less water than the same plant in a clay pot.
- A plant that has recently been repotted needs less water than a plant with roots filling the pot.
- A plant grown in a small pot needs more water than the same plant moved to a larger pot.

The only way to talk about the appropriate water level is to describe it in terms of how damp the soil is. And you measure that degree of dampness with a tool you always have with you: your finger.

In the encyclopedia section of this book, that proper level of soil moisture is described for each plant. The following terms are used:

Evenly moist	This is the wettest condition of all. It means that the top layer of soil feels like a damp sponge: you thoroughly soaked it, then squeezed out all the water you could, but it's still damp to the touch.
Lightly moist	That same sponge, a few hours later; a little bit damp, but starting to dry.
Dry an inch down	Poke your finger down into the soil at the edge of the pot (less danger of breaking a root there); what does it feel like?

For plants that don't need a lot of water, like succulents and cacti, sometimes you are told to water only when the plant is "almost completely dry." It's a little tricky to tell when that is, because it's not so easy to get your finger that far down in a pot, especially with a thorny cactus. Here's another technique. With the business end of a kitchen fork, dig down near the edge of the pot at least halfway through the soil. Then pull the dirt back with the tines of the fork and put your finger down into this temporary hole. If it's damp, wait a day or so and try again. When you finally find dry soil halfway down, pick up the pot and try to memorize how heavy it feels. Next time, you can judge dryness by weight and skip the fork test.

You can also use a wooden chopstick (which, by the way, is handy for lots of plant chores). Insert it down into the soil, leave it for a minute or so, and then pull it out and "read" it like the dipstick in your car. A little bit of wet soil will probably cling to the chopstick, whereas the dry part won't. It's a little less precise than using your finger, but better than nothing.

If you're very uncertain, or for some reason want to know the *exact* moisture content of your soil, you can buy a gauge in most large plant shops. You stick one of these devices down into the soil at various depths, and it measures the moisture there and shows a reading with a needle on a gauge.

How to Water Correctly

You can water any plant from either the top or the bottom; even though most people think of pouring water into the top of the pot, there are situations where bottom watering is preferable.

Top watering. There's a right way and a wrong way. Now's the time to develop good habits.

- Use a watering can with a long spout. That way, you'll be able to put the water where you want it—on the soil—and not where you don't want it, on the leaves or spilled on the floor. Leaves of some plants are damaged if water gets on them, so you have a choice: you can either learn which plants have this problem and which don't, or you can just get in the habit of avoiding the leaves all the time—whichever you think is easier.
- Use lots of water. Keep pouring until water runs out the drainage hole in the bottom. If you add only a little dribble of water, just enough to dampen the top, the roots will reach up to where the water is, and the plant will not develop fully. Note, however, that if water comes right out the drainage hole as fast as you pour it in, you have a problem: the soil is not taking up any water at all. See "full soak" technique below.
- Drain off the excess that collects in the drainage saucer. Don't let the water sit there, or it will be absorbed back into the soil from the bottom, and then the roots will have too much water. This is the way root rot starts.
- Don't use very cold water. This is stressful for some plants, and less of a problem for others.
- Fluoride can cause the leaves of some plants to turn brown on the tips. If your municipal water supply has added fluoride, let the water sit in the watering can overnight.

Bottom watering. Certain plants can rot if their leaves get wet; fuzzy leaves are particularly susceptible. To avoid the possibility of accidental spills, a technique of watering from the bottom has been developed. It can be used for any plant, but most often will probably be used for African violets.

Bottom watering involves nothing more than filling the drip saucer with water and allowing the soil to draw in the water through the drainage hole. It's a slow process, but eventually enough water will be absorbed that the top of the soil feels damp when you touch it. This method is more successful with clay pots than with plastic.

Bottom watering is recommended for plants with fuzzy leaves, like African violets, which can rot if water gets on their leaves.

Wick watering. This is a variation of bottom watering. A wick of some absorbent fabric is inserted down through the soil and out through the drainage hole. The wick sits in a reservoir of water, and draws water up into the soil. The reservoir can be either just under the pot, or off to the side. For small plants, the saucer that came with the pot is probably sufficient; larger plants will need a deeper saucer.

In a plant store you may see something labeled a "self-watering pot." It's a wick system: a pot with a wick on top of a large water-holding reservoir.

You can make your own wicking pot; they are especially good for times when you'll be away for several weeks. Use soft fabric that is made of natural fibers like cotton or linen (not polyester; it doesn't wick well); a strip torn from an old T-shirt or diaper is perfect, or you can use the wick meant for oil lamps.

Using a pencil or chopstick, push one end of the wick through the drainage hole up into the soil as far as you can. Let some of the wick dangle out through the hole. Put the pot into a deep saucer and fill the saucer with water. You can also put water into a nearby container, as long as you make sure the wick reaches to the bottom of the water container. This is a way to wick-water several plants from one reservoir.

A wicking system draws water up into the soil continuously and gradually. Here the pot sits on a bed of pebbles, filled halfway with water; this will keep the soil lightly moist with no danger of overwatering. Ready-made "self-watering pots" use the wicking principle. Homemade or store-bought, wick watering systems are good choices for people who are away from home for long periods.

Full soak. This is an emergency measure, for those times when a plant has been completely neglected and the leaves are totally drooped. If the soil and root ball are completely dry, you won't be able simply to add water in the normal way. The soil has pulled away from the edge of the pot, and the top layer is hard and compacted, so the water will run right out without being absorbed into the soil.

Fill a large container—a bucket, say, or your kitchen sink—with water. Put the entire pot in the bucket, up to its rim. If it floats, you may have to hold it down for a few minutes, until it starts to absorb some water. Carefully scratch the surface of the soil, so water can penetrate; a fork or a knitting needle is a good tool.

Keep the pot underwater until air bubbles stop forming and the soil is really damp through and through. When it's ready, the pot should feel heavy, and a little drip should be coming through the drainage hole.

This process works better if the plant happens to be in a clay pot, which will absorb some water through the sides. But you can also do it with plastic pots—and should, if you've got a plant in serious trouble.

Tools for Watering
A watering can with a long spout is necessary. In the shops you will see an assortment of other tools and gadgets related to watering; whether or not you need them is a matter of personal choice, and personal pocketbook.

- A moisture meter that reads soil moisture and registers it with a needle on a gauge.
- Self-watering pots are essentially wicking systems; they are useful for vacation times.
- Water-retaining polymers are little beads of absorbent material that you add into your potting mix so they are distributed throughout the soil. They absorb water, in the process assuming a jellylike consistency, and release the water gradually into the soil. At least that's the theory; experts disagree on their effectiveness.

Watering Checklist
√ Water according to the needs of the plant, not according to the calendar.
√ Feel the soil to see how dry it is; you can't tell by looking.
√ Water thoroughly, until water runs out the bottom; pour out whatever collects in the drain saucer.
√ Don't pour water directly onto leaves unless you know it doesn't bother the plant.

√ Brown leaves and wilted leaves mean you need more water. Yellow leaves on bottom mean you're watering too much.

√ If you're not sure whether it's time to water, wait a day or two. Less is definitely better than more.

Light

Light is absolutely essential for growing plants. A plant manufactures its food by a chemical process that starts when sunlight hits the leaves and interacts with the chlorophyll in them. (Chlorophyll is what makes the leaves green.) If the light that reaches the plant is insufficient, the plant cannot make food for itself and therefore cannot grow.

The ill effects of inadequate light may take a long time to show up. If light conditions are very poor, the plant will die; if they are marginal, the plant will hang on but not thrive. On the other hand, too much light can also be a problem; many plants will simply burn up if they are put in direct sunlight. This damage—brown patches on the leaves—shows up much faster.

The Right Amount of Light

As with other aspects of care, plants have an inborn need for a certain level of light, depending on their native environments. Those that grow naturally in forests or heavy jungles are used to sunlight mixed with shadow; desert plants are used to full sunlight all day long. Fortunately for us, many of the plant species that are used as houseplants are very tough; they will adapt to indoor light conditions that may be less than ideal.

When you acquire a plant that is new to you, take a minute to read about the light conditions it requires. Different levels of light are described with these terms:

Full sun   This means that the rays of the sun come through the window and fall directly on the plant.

Filtered light   This means that the plant is near a window that gets strong sun, but there is something between the sun's rays and the plant, like a sheer curtain, that acts as a filter.

Indirect light   This means that the sun's rays come through the window unimpeded, but they don't fall directly on the plant; they bounce off something like a mirror or a wall.

Filtered light and indirect light are about the same, as far as the plant is concerned: a medium level.

Semishady   The corners of the room get very little bright light, either directly or indirectly; this describes the lowest level of light a plant can tolerate.

No plant can live in corners that get no light at all. If you're considering a location you're not sure about, on a sunny day hold your hand up where the plant will be. If it casts a faint shadow, you can grow a low-light plant there. If there's no shadow at all, find another spot.

You can grow plants in very dim areas if you are able occasionally to move them into brighter spots for a while. Using a rotation system, it is possible to have plants in spots with no windows at all, like a hallway or stairwell.

Sun Movements
Often you read or hear someone say, "Put the plant in an east window"—or south, or north, or west. What's that all about?

The intensity of the sun changes during the day, as you know if you've ever gotten a sunburn by staying on the beach too long in the middle of the day. In the early morning, it's less intense; it gets more intense near the middle of the day, then gradually less intense in the afternoon. So a window that faces east, where the sun is in the morning, gets sunlight that is less powerful, whereas a window that faces south would receive the brightest, most intense sunlight of the day.

Of course you must use your common sense about this. If the window that faces south is blocked by a large shade tree or by a nearby building, less light is going to come into your room. But as a general guideline:

North window	Least light
East window	Next brightest
West window	Next brightest
South window	Brightest of all

Another thing to take into consideration is the changes in the sun's path at different times of the year. In winter, the sun's arc through the sky is much lower than the summer circuit, so sunlight comes in the window at a different angle.

In winter, we get less sunshine inside. Happily, most plants are in a kind of resting period then, not actively growing, and the lower light does not present a setback. If your plant grows well in the summer, chances are it's getting the right amount of light and you can just leave it there all year long.

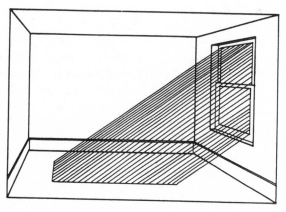

In winter, the sun travels across the sky at a low angle. Winter sunbeams coming through a window are less intense and are dispersed over a larger area, so indoor plants get less light.

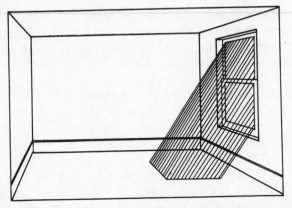

The summer sun makes a broader arc than the winter sun, and light comes through a window at a higher angle. In these much more intense, concentrated sunbeams, plants can burn.

Artificial Light

Many people who are into houseplants in a big way soon run out of good spaces to put plants, and compensate by installing some kind of artificial lights. This represents a financial investment that ranges from modest to substantial, and even more it represents an emotional commitment. It says you are ready to modify your house for the benefit of your plants.

First of all, incandescent lights (the normal light bulbs) won't help much. They put out much more heat than light, and if a plant is close enough to a lamp to get any light benefit, it's also getting way too hot. The only lights that are good for plants are fluorescents. You can use either regular fluorescent fixtures and bulbs, or stands made just for plants that hold special "grow-light" bulbs.

If you already have fluorescent light fixtures in a room, you're in luck. You're especially in luck if they hold two bulbs. The best arrangement for plants is one "cool white" bulb and one "warm white." Manufacturers sometimes create other names for these two types, but the salesperson in the store should be able to help you get one of each. The cool white bulb has light at the blue end of the color spectrum; blue light is what plants need to make leaves and stems grow. The warm white bulb has light at the red end of the spectrum; plants use red light to grow roots.

Fixtures made especially for growing plants have some of both colors in their bulbs; the blue and red together produce a bright purple light that some people find unattractive. Newer fixtures have bulbs that produce both kinds of light, but the visual effect is more like natural daylight.

Unless you're working toward a special effect, don't keep your plants under lights twenty-four hours a day. In the outdoors they have a period of darkness, and they need it indoors too.

Plants and Sunshine

Plants naturally grow toward the source of light. Sometimes you see a plant that is very obviously leaning off to one side; it is stretching toward its light. To keep the plant looking balanced, give it a quarter turn every week or so.

Two rules of thumb to keep in mind:

1. Plants that produce flowers will flower only if they receive enough light. They may live quite well in less light, but they won't flower.
2. Plants that have variegated leaves (meaning there are areas of white or yellow mixed in with the green) need more light than all-green varieties. That's because there is no chlorophyll in the white areas of the leaf, and so the plant has less chlorophyll available for food manufacture. To compensate, the plant needs more sunshine.

Light Checklist

√ Flowering plants need light to make flower buds.
√ Variegated plants need more light.
√ The amount of light in any one spot changes with the time of day and with the season.
√ Artificial lights should be fluorescent, and should combine warm white and cool white bulbs.

Humidity

Why does your prayer plant have brown circles at the tips of the leaves? Why are the outer edges of your fern turning brown? Why did the African violet make so many buds that never opened? Because they're not getting enough humidity. Lack of humidity in itself won't kill your plants, but it keeps them from thriving, and the effects are ugly.

Humidity means the moisture in the air. Humidity is what makes your windows fog up when you're boiling water; the heat is changing some of the water in the pot to water vapor, which is water in gas form rather than liquid.

In the jungle, the soil and the leaves of all the plants catch water, which slowly and continually evaporates into the air as water vapor; the atmosphere is constantly humid. So plants that thrive in tropical or semitropical environments have a built-in need for high humidity—higher than our modern, centrally heated homes usually have.

Therefore, if you have humidity-loving plants in your house, you'll have to create humid conditions for them. Fortunately, you don't have to do anything drastic to the whole house, or the whole room; there are ways to humidify the air right around the plant.

Ways to Increase Humidity

Spray. Spray a fine mist of water on and around the plant. You can buy misters in the store, or use an empty household spray bottle. Spritz all around the plant; when you're done, a fine mist should be on all the leaves.

For sensitive plants, you may have to do this every day, especially in the summer. If you have several plants that need misting, in different rooms of the house, get several different spray bottles. If the mister is right nearby, you're much more likely to use it.

Don't spray plants whose leaves are damaged by water drops, such as African violets.

Keep plants on a pebble tray. Fill a wide, shallow container with small rocks, then fill the container with water not quite up to the top of the rocks; refill to keep the water at that level. The plant will sit on top of the rocks, and you don't want the pot sitting in water.

As the water evaporates, it creates a mini-environment right around the plant that is extra humid. Remember that water vapor goes straight up, so the pebble tray should be as wide across as the plant's leaf span; something small won't work.

A pebble tray is for plants that need high levels of humidity. Keep it filled halfway with water. The evaporating water creates a humid environment right around the plant.

To keep the water from taking on a sour smell, tuck in a few pieces of charcoal (not the kind you barbecue your hamburgers with; the plant store sells small bags of tiny charcoal bits).

The tray itself can be anything watertight that is deep enough. You can use old baking pans or platters (if they have any kind of lip); look around your kitchen or keep an eye out at the next yard sale. In plant stores you can buy large drainage saucers (separate from the pot), and they make wonderful pebble trays. Plastic saucers are best for this purpose; they hold water longer. Clay saucers are handsome, but they are not watertight; if you want to use one, coat the inside with shellac or some other kind of sealer.

----------------------- -----------------------

Decorating Tip

To highlight an extra-special plant, use special pebbles. Clear or colored glass marbles can be purchased in florist shops. If you live in the country near a stream, collect small river rocks. Look for pretty ones in the same colors; they will be polished smooth by the running water. Or use small rocks you collected on your family vacation; if you know someone who has a rock polisher, ask your friend to polish them for you.

----------------------- -----------------------

Group plants together. As part of the natural cycle, plants give off water vapor through their leaves. If you cluster groups of plants close together, they can humidify each other. If your pebble tray is large enough, you can group several pots on one pebble tray, and get humidity in both ways.

A large pebble tray can hold several plants. They get a double dose of humidity: from the evaporating water, and from the water vapor that the nearby plants transpire through their leaves.

When you arrange your groupings, be aware of what looks good together. Also, think about the other conditions that the

plants need. You'll want plants that have compatible needs for
light, and your life will be easier if they also need the same
kind of watering.

Surround plants with wet moss. Choose a container that
is big enough to hold the plant (or plants; you can use groupings here too) with room to spare. Arrange a single layer of
pebbles, or a saucer upside down, or a small piece of wood—
anything that will lift the pot up off the bottom of the container
so that it never sits directly in water. Put the plant, in its pot,
into the container.

Another way to provide humidity is to pack the pots inside a larger pot filled
with something that retains water for a long time and slowly evaporates it
into the air around the plant. Vermiculite, shown here, is one substance; you
can also use sphagnum moss.

In the plant store you can buy a bag of sphagnum moss;
it's that gray-green stuff that looks like tangled-up knitting
yarn. Fill a bucket or pan with water and put in as much moss
as you think you're going to need; hold it under until it gets
really wet. Then pack the wet moss in all around the plant's
pot. The idea is that the moss will hold water for a long time,
and it will gradually evaporate in the surrounding air. As the
moss gets dry, add more water (spraying is a good way).
    With this technique, you can use deeper containers than you

For extra humidity, group several plants together in a large bed of vermiculite or peat moss. They benefit from each other's transpiration, as well as water evaporation.

would for a pebble tray—brass planters, pretty ceramic pots, whatever. This is a good way to feature a special plant in a special container.

Keep the plant under glass. A terrarium—any large glass container with a top that closes—creates an environment that

High-humidity plants do well (and look pretty) in an open terrarium, which helps hold moisture inside. Be sure to provide adequate drainage; here a layer of pebbles keeps plants' roots away from any standing water.

is constantly humid because water vapor can't escape. You can create a modified terrarium for humidity-loving plants by planting them in glass bowls or jars that have a narrower opening at the top; a brandy snifter, for instance, with one exquisite African violet.

If you put the plant directly into the glass container, you must be very careful to provide good drainage. Look in chapter 8 for more details on how to plant a terrarium. A safer method is to keep the plant in its original pot, put something in the bottom of the glass container that will lift the plant's pot slightly, and fill in all around with a disguising layer of moss.

Keep plants in humid rooms. All other things being equal, plants that love humidity are better off in rooms that are humid: the kitchen and the bathroom. The humidity created by frequent showers, or by steaming pots, will make the plants very happy. So if the light and temperature in those two rooms are appropriate for the plants, find a spot for them. It's a nice way to dress up a bathroom.

There are other good reasons to keep plants in the bathroom or kitchen. Both have sinks, which are a perfect place to water your plants; just turn on the tap and let the water run through, letting the excess run safely into the sink.

Humidity Checklist

✓ Brown leaf tips are usually a sign that the humidity is too low. Take corrective action.

✓ Check your system regularly: does the pebble tray need more water; is the moss dry?

✓ Plants that need very high levels of humidity will benefit from a combination of techniques: in glass and surrounded by moss, or grouped together and surrounded by moss, or kept in the bathroom and sprayed regularly.

And both provide you a handy way to wash the plants. Put the plants in the kitchen sink and spray them all over with the sprayer attachment. In the bathroom, take them all into the shower and give them a communal rinse.

Temperature

Most houseplants like the same temperatures that people do. This means that by and large, temperature is not a problem you have to worry about.

The plants from the tropics—and that's most of them—are happy with daytime temperatures in the range of 65 to 70 degrees, and a bit cooler at night . . . just like us. You don't have to be concerned about keeping the same temperature twenty-four hours a day; after all, in their natural environment it gets cooler when the sun goes down.

There are a few plants that simply do better with temperatures a bit cooler than we would consider comfortable (check the descriptions in the encyclopedia section). For those plants, find a permanent place in your home that is naturally cooler—perhaps a room on the north side of the house, or a bedroom you don't heat as much.

Be aware that the glass in windows gets very cold at night in the wintertime. Be sure that no leaves actually touch the glass, or they could literally freeze.

Plants like fresh air. In everything but very cold weather, a gentle breeze through an open door is good for your houseplants. But cold drafts are another story. Lots of plants are killed because they are put in an entranceway, where cold air hits them every time the front door is opened.

Fertilizing

When we add fertilizer to plants, we're not really "feeding" them. Plants make their own food, using sunlight and chlorophyll in the leaves to produce carbohydrates. In order for this manufacturing process to take place, however, plants need certain minerals; these minerals are part of the chemical formula of photosynthesis.

Minerals are present naturally in soil outdoors, and they are present in potting soil that we use to pot our plants with. But over time, they get used up and need to be replaced. That's where fertilizer comes in.

Choosing Fertilizer

When you go to the store to buy some fertilizer, you will notice that it comes in lots of forms but that every package prominently shows three numbers, like this:

8 - 20 - 10

The numbers indicate the proportion of the three main minerals in the fertilizer, always in the same order.

Nitrogen   This is the first number. Nitrogen produces healthy leaves.

Phosphorus   This is the second number. Phosphorus helps plants produce strong cells, and has an effect on overall health, including flowering.

Potassium   This is the third number. Potassium (also called potash) helps plants flower and develop strong root systems.

For most houseplants, you want a formula in a relative proportion of 1:2:1, such as 5-10-5, or 10-20-10. If flowers are your main concern, choose a fertilizer with high second and third numbers; if you're concerned about the leaves, get a fertilizer with a high first number.

Your second decision will be the physical type of fertilizer. Several forms are available.

- Powders or concentrated liquids; these are meant to be dissolved in water.
- Concentrated beads or tablets that are to be dispersed throughout the potting soil; they release the fertilizer slowly as they gradually dissolve with the water you add to the pot.

- Granules that are meant to be scattered over the surface of the soil and scratched in.
- Short sticks of compressed fertilizer; these are slow-release formulas, like the beads. Use a pencil to push them way down into the soil, near the edge of the pot.

The kind mixed in water seems to be what most people choose, probably because they take care of two tasks—watering and fertilizing—at one time. That doesn't mean, however, that you fertilize every time you water.

When and How to Fertilize

The question of how is determined by the kind of fertilizer you purchase. Whichever form you choose, read the directions on the package carefully, and *follow them*. A double dose is not twice as good; it can do real damage to the plant.

The question of when is a bit trickier. In general, plants need fertilizing the most when they're actively growing. Many plants have a natural resting period in the winter, and you should stop fertilizing then. Start your fertilizing program in the spring, when the plant is ready to put on a spurt of growth.

If your plant is one that flowers, fertilize lightly all during the flowering season. Many people keep flowers coming on for a long time by giving the plant a very thinly diluted drink of fertilizer with every watering in spring and summer.

Commercial greenhouses fertilize heavily, to promote rapid growth. When you purchase a new plant, you can be sure it has recently gotten a big dose of fertilizer and won't need any more for two or three months. In fact, it's a good idea to flush the soil when you first bring a new plant home. To do this, set the pot in the kitchen sink and let lots of water run through it.

Also remember that when you repot a plant, you're putting it in fresh soil that already has minerals in it; don't fertilize for several months.

If you see white crusty patches on top of the soil, or white or green scum on the outside of your clay pots, those are buildups of fertilizer salts, the solid residue from minerals dissolved in water. If this shows up in the first year or so, it could be a sign that you're fertilizing too heavily. Scrape off the crusty parts and replace with new soil, and adjust your fertilizing schedule downward.

In general terms, fertilizing is not a life-and-death issue with houseplants, not in the same way that water and light are. Most of the time, the soil has enough minerals already in it to maintain plants. They may not grow picture-perfect, but they will maintain. If you get in the habit of adding fertilizer once a month in the spring and summer, most plants will be fine.

Fertilizing Checklist

√ If lower leaves on plants turn yellow and you're certain you're watering properly, this could be a sign of mineral deficiency. Are you fertilizing?

√ Follow directions on the package. You can give a weaker dose than the directions call for, but not stronger.

√ Fertilizer is not medicine. If your plant is doing poorly because of bad light or a disease, fertilizing will only make matters worse. First fix the basic problem.

Pruning

All other things being equal, pruning will not keep your plants alive, and the lack of pruning will not kill them. It's a question of how the plant looks. But with plants, appearance is everything. When you think about it, the reason we have indoor plants in the first place is the visual pleasure they add to our lives.

Pruning—cutting away some part of the plant—is what will keep your plants from getting scraggly, scrawny, and "leggy"—which means all stretched out with long pieces of bare stem between leaves. The actual technique of pruning isn't at all difficult. The hard part is convincing yourself to do it. The problem is that the part you prune out and discard always looks so *healthy*; you feel like a murderer. Take heart: the plant will recover quickly and will definitely look better. Besides, you can always take the prunings and start new baby plants from them.

Why Bother with Pruning?

Pruning is the way you keep your houseplant in a nice balanced, symmetrical shape. Not all plants need it; some grow in such a way that they stay looking nice all on their own. Others grow every which way and get out of control fast.

Plants get out of shape for several reasons:

- They grow toward the light, and if you don't turn them every now and then, they'll become lopsided.
- Some are basically vines that grow long and skinny instead of short and bushy.
- They've been fertilized incorrectly or irregularly.
- They're contrary; for no reason that you can see, one side of the plant grows faster.

With skillful pruning, you can bring a lopsided plant back into balance. You can also direct the plant to grow into a certain shape and configuration.

The Basic Pruning Principle

Plants grow from the top, not from the bottom. Here's a way to remember this: Let's say you plant a small apple tree in your backyard, and nail a metal name tag to the trunk five feet from the ground. Ten years later the tree is much, much taller, but the name tag is still in the same place, still five feet from the ground.

If you wanted your apple tree to grow tall instead of wide, you'd just let it go, maybe taking off some of the lower branches. But if you wanted a low tree with lots of branches (so you could reach the apples), you would take off the growing tip at the very top of the tree. That will not kill the tree; it will only force the growth energy downward to the next set of buds, the ones that produce side branches.

The topmost bud will produce a new stretch of main stem. In many plants, the lower two buds will never develop. The plant will continue to grow in one upright direction.

The basic principle works with houseplants too:

- If you want the plant to grow short and bushy, prune out the top.
- If you want the plant to grow tall and thin, prune off the side branches.

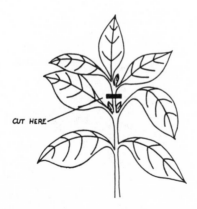

If the top section containing the leading bud is removed, the two lower buds will develop into side branches. The plant will then have a wider silhouette.

To create a tall, vertical plant, you may have to remove any side branches that develop.

With most houseplants, that is. Some plants produce just one main stem and will never branch. If the top of the stem is cut off, a new single stem forms in its place. You can't force palms to branch, for instance, and you shouldn't try. But in general, you can shape your plants to grow the way you want.

To create a rounded, bushy shape, prune away the top, where the growing tip is. For more fullness, pinch off the tips of all side branches.

Pruning to Control Shape

Sometimes it is as simple as cutting off a branch that is spoiling the shape of a plant. With a sharp knife, scissors, or small pruning shears, cut off the branch back to the point where symmetry is restored.

Pruning is needed to get a lopsided plant back into balance. Don't be afraid to cut off branches that spoil the overall shape of the plant.

And sometimes it's a never-ending process. That's because the plant has a natural urge to grow in a straight line, like the vine it really is; unless you step in, it will grow one long trailing stem all around the room.

Wandering jew is a classic example. If you want a full, rounded shape, you must continually keep removing the growing tip. The buds lower down on the stem, just below where you cut, will become side branches. Once they start to grow, if you take off *their* tips, they'll divide once again. It's a continual process: as the side stems grow, keep pruning and you'll have a plant with a nice rounded shape instead of lanky and spindly.

You need to start this process early, when the plant is just beginning to reach over the rim of the pot. The stem will branch just at the point where you cut. So if you let your wandering jew grow down to a length of two feet before you prune it, you'll always have the two feet of single stem.

Green Thumb Tip

Say your wandering jew has wandered too far, and you're in the mood to prune but not fuss too much. Take the snippets that you prune off and stick them right back into the pot with the mother plant, without going to the trouble of rooting them first. Some of them will take root directly. The ones that don't will eventually dry up and turn brown, and you can dispose of them with a clear conscience.

Techniques and Tools

Many houseplants have a soft stem that you can pinch with your fingers, and that's why the most common pruning technique is called "pinching"—you just reach right in and pinch out the topmost growing part.

"Pinching" means removing the growing tip; if the stems are soft, you can just pinch it off with your fingers. Vines like wandering jew and philodendron need continual pinching so they don't get scraggly.

If the stems of your plant are a bit too tough to pinch with your fingers, use a razor blade, knife, or scissors. But be careful that you cut only what you want. There are small pruning tools meant just for houseplants; the cutting edge is short so you don't accidentally cut more than you meant to.

Pruning for legginess. We say a plant is leggy when it has lots of space between sets of leaves. It gets leggy when it's not getting enough light; the stems are reaching for the sunlight, and you end up with long segments of bare stems between leaves. This won't hurt the plant, but it's not attractive.

First, cut or pinch back the stems to the point where they start to get leggy. No matter what you do, those bare stems won't fill in with leaves, so you have to get rid of the leggy parts.

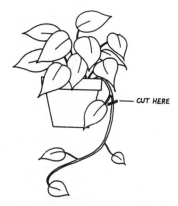

This plant has gotten leggy—too much stem, too few leaves. Prune off the leggy section back to where the leaves are tight. You can root cuttings from the section you removed.

Next, find a better spot for the plant, one with better light. Then, if you want to, you can make cuttings out of the part you cut off and start some baby plants (see chapter 7).

Pruning a too-tall plant. Plants with one main trunk that has gotten too tall, with all the leaves bunched at the top, look top-heavy. Dracaenas are especially vulnerable to this, because they naturally drop their lower leaves as they grow

304

taller. There's nothing you can do to make the plant replace the leaves lower down on the trunk; the only remedy is to shorten the trunk and start over.

If the trunk is hard and woody, which it probably is, you'll have to use a sharp, heavy knife or strong pruning shears. Choose the point where you want new leaves to begin, and cut there. Be patient; it takes a while before new growth sprouts. The part you cut off can be rooted for a new plant; see chapter 7.

This dracaena has too much stem for its few leaves.

Decide how long a stem you would like a new plant to have, and cut there; you'll need a sharp knife. You can start another plant with the part you cut off; see chapter 7.

Treat the plant just as you did when it had leaves, and you may be rewarded eventually with new growth at the point where you cut.

You should know that this procedure, like any surgery, is not without risk. What you have done is taken off all the leaves, which the plant needs to produce its food. If there's enough food energy stored in the stem and roots to keep the plant alive until new leaves sprout, all is well. If not . . .

A safer way to deal with those long, bare stems is the technique called "air layering," which is explained in chapter 7. It's more trouble, but you're less likely to have a corpse on your hands. Here's where your common sense comes in: if the plant is really awful looking, so bad you're considering tossing it out, you have little to lose by simply cutting it way back.

Pruning Checklist

√ If you're constantly fighting legginess, your plant needs a different location, with better light.

√ With trailing and climbing plants that need regular pinching, be very watchful in spring and summer; they're growing fast then.

√ The best time for major pruning is early spring or late summer.

Good Grooming

Keeping Plants Clean

In your home, plants collect dust at the same rate every other surface does—too fast. But while dust simply looks icky on the furniture, on the plants it actually causes harm.

For one thing, dust blocks sunlight from the leaves so the process of photosynthesis is sluggish. (By the way, dirty windows have the same effect on your plants.) For another, accumulated dust will clog the pores on the surface of the leaves, so they don't "breathe" normally.

Perhaps the biggest concern is harmful insects. Spider mites, one of the most difficult problems to deal with, seem to love dusty environments. Keeping plants clean is one way to keep disease conditions under control.

- Most plants can be cleaned by gentle spraying with the hose outdoors (if the weather is warm) or by the hose attachment on the kitchen sink (if it's cold outside).
- If the plant is too big to move to the sink, wipe each leaf individually with a soapy sponge, then rinse with clear water.
- An easy way to do several plants at one time is to move them all into the shower.
- To clean a small plant with tiny leaves, turn the whole thing upside down and swish it through a pail of soapy water; follow with a clear-water rinse.
- Plants with fuzzy leaves are *very* susceptible to collecting dust, and *very* difficult to clean. Because fuzzy leaves tend to spot or rot if water gets on them, you can't wash them in any normal way. Solution: brush off the dust. Use a soft paintbrush or clean makeup brush.

Grooming

All plants need a certain amount of tidying up. It's part of the natural cycle that old leaves die as new ones are being born. Don't let the dead leaves stay on the plant or on the soil; they foster disease.

If for any of several reasons a leaf develops a problem area—a sunburn spot, brown tips, fertilizer burns—you should get in there with your scissors and trim off the ugly part. A leaf will never regenerate the tip you cut off, but at least it looks better. When you trim, cut in such a way that the natural shape of the leaf is maintained. One of the ugliest sights, and most common, is leaf tips trimmed off with a straight cut.

5

What's Wrong
with My Plant?

Plants get sick, just as people do. They catch a cold, get a virus, become malnourished. Harmful insects attack them and wreak havoc. But their greatest enemy of all is people. Human beings cause more harm to plants than all the insects and diseases combined.

Unfortunately, a sick plant has only a few ways of communicating its ills. Several very different conditions will show themselves with the same symptom. If the leaves of your plant turn brown on the edges, that could be a sign of too much water. Or too little. Or too much fertilizer. Or too little humidity. Or too much direct sunlight. It's not possible to say, in simple black-and-white terms, that symptom X is caused by situation Y and the solution is Z.

Commonsense Guideline
Make your best guess about the problem, take corrective action, give the plant a month to improve, and see what happens. If you lose the plant, give it a decent burial and buy another one. Life goes on.

310

This can be very, very frustrating for plant owners. You can spend lots of valuable time trying to diagnose the problem, and even more valuable energy worrying and fretting, only to have the plant die anyway.

If one of your plants starts looking puny, you have to become a detective. Look first at the conditions it is living in; review what you've been doing, and compare that with the symptoms described in this chapter. At the same time, examine the plant for insects and disease.

Human Mistakes

What You Did	The Results
Too much water	Bottom leaves turn yellow. Tips of leaves turn brown. Entire plant droops. Leaves drop. Plant shows patches of something that looks like mildew. The base of the stem, at the soil line, is soft and mushy. Roots are rotting.
Too little water	Plant droops. Leaves curl under and edges turn brown. Leaves fall off. Stunted growth. Flower buds fall off before they open.
Too much light	Brown or washed-out patches on the leaves (burn marks). Edges of leaves are brown.
Too little light	Stems are leggy. Plant is turning yellow. Plant is lopsided, reaching for light.

What You Did	*The Results*
Too little light (*continued*)	New leaves on a variegated plant are reverting to all green.
	New leaves are smaller than older ones.
	Flowering plants don't flower.
Too much fertilizer	New growth is lanky and leggy.
	Edges of leaves turn brown.
	Plants that should flower have lots of leaves but no buds.
Too little fertilizer	New leaves are small.
	Lower leaves turn yellow.
	Entire plant turns yellow and pale.
	Edges of leaves turn brown.
	Plant has stopped growing.
	Yellow or brown patches on leaves.
Too much humidity	Patches of gray mold on leaves or stems.
Too little humidity	Edges and tips of leaves turn brown.
	Flower buds don't open.
Too cold	Leaves turn yellow, fall off.
	Edges of leaves curl under.
	Plant seems to stop growing.
	Flower buds fall off before they open.
Too warm	Leaves turn brown at tips or edges.
	Flowers bloom but die off very fast.
	Plant droops.
Drafts	Leaves drop off.
	Edges of leaves turn brown.

Insects and Disease

Although these problems are less common than "people" mistakes, houseplants are sometimes infested with insects or disease. That kind of trouble is contagious, so if you suspect an insect infestation, isolate the plant while you work on it. The flip side is that the problem probably came from another plant in the first place, either in the grower's greenhouse or nearby outdoor plants. Therefore:

• When you bring a new plant home, watch closely for insects the first few days. If possible, keep the plant away from your other plants during that time.
• If you put your plants outside in the garden or on the balcony during the summer, check them very carefully when you bring them back in.

Insect Controls

The best control is prevention. Learn whether the plants you have are especially vulnerable to a certain insect, and what conditions discourage it. Keep your plants clean and free of dust. Remove dead leaves from the plant and the soil; decaying leaves are a breeding ground for trouble.

But if you are visited by these little devils in spite of your efforts, there are ways to handle the problem. The first thing is to move the patient away from your other plants so they don't become infected too.

Start with nonpoisonous methods: wash or scrape bugs off or dab them with a cotton swab dipped in rubbing alcohol. If that doesn't work, use an insecticide. Remember that insecticides are poisons. Be careful of the environment—the one inside your home as well as the larger world outside. Read labels; ask for advice in a shop you trust.

These are some of the names you will see on the labels of commercial pesticides:

- *Rotenone, pyrethrin, pyrethrum.* All three of these are made from plant materials, and they degrade relatively quickly into harmless compounds. They are all effective against the kinds of insects that affect houseplants.
- *Malathion.* This is an organic phosphate, and fairly safe.
- *Cygon, diazinon, sevin.* All are much stronger than the first group of three; use with extreme care.
- *Isotox.* A systemic poison (meaning it works on the whole plant) that is dissolved in water and taken in by the roots.
- *Nicotine sulfate.* A highly toxic substance derived from tobacco; use very carefully.

All insecticides are poisons. Unless it's too big to move, take the plant outside to spray it. You don't want to breathe the fumes. If you have to spray very large plants that are too big to move, at least open several windows.

The most common kinds of insects are described below.

Aphids

If you have an outdoor garden, you already know what aphids look like. They are tiny little things, about as big as the head

Aphids are small but not so tiny you can't see them. This is a typical thick infestation: they're crawling all over each other.

of a pin, either light green or black. They suck the juices of new growth, and so you will find them mostly at the growing tips of your plants, bunched on top of each other.

The damage. Quite literally, they suck the life out of the plant. The new leaves will begin to look twisted and deformed; they never develop into mature healthy leaves. Eventually, the whole plant dies.

The evidence. You can see these critters with the naked eye. Look at the buds and the newest leaves. Another clue: the leaves feel sticky, and so does the furniture the plant is sitting on. If the table feels sticky when you dust it, look for aphids.

The solution. First try knocking them off by spraying the plant *hard* with a garden hose or kitchen-sink sprayer; repeat if needed. If that doesn't work, spray with insecticide. Trim off the buds or leaves that are deformed; when the plant produces new growth, be on the lookout.

Mealybugs

If the whole plant is taking on a yellow appearance, and the leaves are shriveled and deformed, you may have a mealybug problem.

The damage. Like aphids, these are sucking insects that gradually drain the life out of a plant. African violets and piggyback plants are especially vulnerable.

The evidence. The insects themselves are small, but they cover themselves with a white wool that is very visible; they look like miniature balls of cotton candy. They are on tops or bottoms of leaves, or in the joints.

Mealybugs are small but cover themselves with a white fluffy "wool" that makes them visible.

The solution. Dip a cotton swab in denatured alcohol and dab the bugs with it; wash the plant with soapy water to get rid of the dead bodies. This will work if you just have a few, but a serious case of mealybug is very difficult to eradicate. You're better off to discard the plant.

Red Spider Mites

Also called just "red spider" or "spider mites," these insects are the most difficult to get rid of. The smartest thing is to prevent the problem from developing in the first place. Red spider loves dry, dusty environments and hates cool, humid ones. Therefore, keep the humidity high and keep the leaves free of dust. Vulnerable plants include schefflera, ivy, and dizygotheca. Be sure to isolate a plant while you're treating it; red spider is easily spread.

The evidence. The mites themselves are so tiny you cannot see them, but they spin tiny webs in the V where leaves and stem join. The leaves show bleached-out, discolored splotches and then start falling off.

The solution. If you see the spiderwebs but no leaf discoloration, you may have caught the problem early. Wash the leaves thoroughly with detergent solution (top and bottom) every few days; watch the plant carefully. If the problem persists, use insecticide; it will probably take one of the strong ones, so be careful. If a month of weekly spraying doesn't cure the problem, get rid of the plant.

Red spider mites spin very small spiderwebs in the notches where leaves join the stem. The insects themselves are too small to see; look for the webs.

Scale
Small insects crawl up the stem of your plant until they find a spot they like, then develop a hard outer shell, rather like a turtle. The shells are usually brown but can also be white or tan. They are small enough that it's easy to mistake them for natural bumpy parts of the stem.

The damage. Leaves turn brown and the entire plant withers, as the insects suck out the juices from the stems.

The evidence. You can see these insects with your naked eye; look on the stems. Often they are bunched up on top of each other.

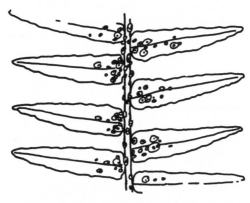

Scale is an insect infestation that attacks ferns, as shown here. Look for small, hard brown or black dots clumped at random on leaves and stems.

The solution. Insecticide sprays don't easily penetrate the hard shell of these insects. You're better off removing them by hand. You can scrape them off with your fingernail or an old toothbrush. If they fall in the soil, remove them. Then scrub the infected stem area with a toothbrush and detergent.

White flies
You know how small fruit flies are, right? They are enormous compared to white flies. This insect is most prevalent with flowering plants.

The damage. Leaves turn yellow. New growth is stunted. Plant gradually declines.

The evidence. The insects themselves are so small you'll never see them, but when you brush against the plant a cloud of white "dust" will suddenly appear as they fly off.

The solution. White fly is hard to fight. For one thing you can't spray the plant, because the insects just fly away before the poison has time to work. The best you can do is wash the plant several times with detergent, or try a systemic poison that goes into the soil.

Pinpointing the Trouble

You have probably noticed that some symptoms appear often in this chapter: yellow leaves, brown edges, stunted growth. If your plant is showing signs of poor health, how can you tell what the trouble is? It's largely a process of elimination, combined with common sense.

1. As a first step, look the plant up in the encyclopedia section (chapter 3). Review the basic conditions that it needs for good health. Also see if it is especially vulnerable to any particular insect disease.
2. Then look carefully at the plant. If you know that this particular plant is, say, often troubled by mealybugs, look for signs of mealybugs.
3. Then look at the environment and review in your mind what you've been doing to take care of the plant. Compare what the plant needs with what you've been giving it, then compare that with the specific trouble indications.

For instance, if you know that the plant needs good light and you can see that it is in a somewhat dim spot, ask yourself if the trouble you're seeing fits the description of too little light. If you read that this plant needs to go dry between waterings, and you realize you've been watering it every three or four days, check the descriptions of damage caused by overwatering.

In the checklist below, common symptoms are described and probable causes suggested. If a symptom has several causes—and most do—the one listed first is the *most* probable.

A Checklist for Sick Plants

The tips of the leaves have turned brown.
- √ Probably indicates that humidity is too low, especially if this is a high-humidity plant.
- √ Could be indication of too much fertilizer, especially if brown is on edges as well as tips.
- √ Also an indication of cold draft.
- √ This is one sign of drought.
- √ It's also a way the plant shows you have been giving it too much water.

The newest leaves are small and look weak.
- √ Not enough light.
- √ Needs fertilizer.
- √ Has become rootbound; needs repotting.

The leaves are pale, the color is faded.
- √ Is the plant getting enough light?
- √ May need fertilizer with a high proportion of nitrogen.

The leaves are curling under.
- √ Look for aphids.

The leaves have spots on them.
- √ Large round brown spots? Probably sunburn. Is plant near a window that gets direct sun?
- √ Irregular-shaped splotches that look as if the green has been bleached out? Check for red spider.
- √ Round white spots? Probably you got water on the leaves when you were watering the plant.

The leaves are turning yellow.
√ If it's the bottom leaves, that's usually a sign of overwatering.
√ If it's scattered, random leaves, check for scale.
√ If it's the youngest leaves, check the root system.
√ Everything slowly turning yellow? Probably not enough light.
√ Insufficient fertilizer.
√ Is this a shade-loving plant? Could be too much light.
√ Are the veins still green on the yellow leaves? Your soil needs iron.
√ Irregular patches of yellow may be caused by lack of nutrients.

When I bought the plant it had variegated leaves, but the ones that have grown since then are solid green.
√ The plant is not getting enough light.

The stems are long and stretched out.
√ Plant needs better light. Move it, then prune off the leggy parts.
√ Have you been fertilizing too much?

The stems are soft and mushy.
√ You're watering too much; probably the roots are damaged too.

The base of the main stem seems rotted.
√ You've been overwatering for a long time; little chance of survival.

The whole plant is wilted.
√ Feel the soil. Is it dry? Give the plant lots of water, enough to soak the root ball.
√ If the soil is wet, you've overwatered. Let the plant dry out, then change your habits.
√ Too much hot sun?

√ Root rot can have this effect; it doesn't show any sign until suddenly the plant keels over. It's terminal.

One day the plant seemed fine, the next day a lot of leaves fell off.

√ Probably it got hit with a cold draft. Is this plant especially vulnerable to drafts?

√ If there's no draft in the room, did the temperature change significantly, especially from cool to warm?

√ If it was only bottom leaves, the plant may need more light.

√ Did you move the plant?

My plant is supposed to flower, but it doesn't.

√ Move to better light.

√ Check your fertilizer; get one with high second and third numbers.

√ Does it need to be cool at night?

6

❦ ❦ ❦

Pots, Soil,
and Repotting

When your children outgrow their sneakers, you buy them bigger shoes. And if the old ones are not worn out, you give them to younger children (if they'll wear them). Same with plants. When they outgrow the pot they're in, you move them into a bigger pot. And you can reuse the old one for another plant; at least your houseplants can't give you any back talk.

People who are new to houseplants are often nervous about repotting a plant. They shouldn't be: the process of repotting does not injure a plant; the plant is going to be so happy to have fresh new soil that it will recover quite nicely from the trauma of being moved. If you really want to worry about something, worry about overwatering or overenthusiastic fertilizing.

In this chapter you will see how easy it is. You will learn how to tell if a plant needs to be repotted, and how to do it, step by step. Then, because this is the natural time to think about pots and soil, you will also learn about:

• different kinds of pots
• the various ingredients of healthy potting soil
• stakes and growing supports
• hanging containers

Pots

When you buy a plant in the store, it comes in a pot (probably plastic) that may or may not have a drip saucer. You can leave it in that pot for a while (unless it's already rootbound when you buy it), or you may want to replace it with something more attractive. But sooner or later, the day will come when you have to move to a bigger container. At that point, you have to make a choice: what kind of pot should you use?

First, a few basics. Pots are measured across the top; a six-inch pot has a diameter of six inches. Often you see newspaper ads from garden centers announcing "six-inch ferns"; it means a fern in a six-inch pot, not a fern with six-inch-long fronds. The one exception is square pots, which are measured across the top on the diagonal.

Standard pots (the vast majority) have the same height as the diameter; a six-inch pot is six inches tall and six inches wide at the top. There is something called an azalea pot, which is only three-fourths as deep as it is wide; there is also a half-pot, for plants with very shallow root systems.

Pots come in a variety of materials.

Types of Pots

Plastic pots. Pots made of plastic offer several advantages. They're lightweight, tough, and inexpensive. They're available almost everywhere and come in a range of sizes and colors. You can even get square ones, which conserve space.

The most important thing to consider is that plastic, by its nature, is waterproof, so it holds in moisture. For moisture-loving plants, that's an advantage; for plants that need dry soil, it's a disaster.

Clay pots. Pots of standard brick red terra-cotta, the familiar clay pots, have been *the* classic for many years. In fact for years they were the only pots, but now they are becoming something of an endangered species. Most plant stores today carry a larger inventory of plastic pots.

Clay pots are heavier than plastic and break more easily; costs are comparable. The key factor about clay is that it is porous; it breathes, which is good for all plants, and it allows water to evaporate through the sides, which is good for some plants but not others. For plants that need dry soil, that are especially susceptible to damage if the roots sit in water, clay is the perfect choice.

Green Thumb Tip

Commonsense rules of thumb for pots:

- Plants that need lots of water—ferns, spathiphyllums—should have plastic pots.
- Plants that need dry soil—cacti, succulents—should have clay pots.
- For everything else, it's a matter of personal choice.

Fiber pots. The horticulture industry uses pots manufactured from a material that is made of pressed fiber; it's gray, with a pebbly texture, and looks a lot like formed cardboard—which is essentially what it is. These pots work fine, but because they are really paper, you should consider them temporary; they will disintegrate in about two years. You may also find pots made of Styrofoam; they too are temporary, because they break so easily.

Decorative pots. You will also see lots of pretty and elegant pots on the shelves—glazed ceramic, brass, what have you. Some of the ceramic pots have drainage holes and saucers, so you can evaluate them the same as plastic (except that they will be much more expensive). Most of the brass and other metal pots are for decorative purposes only; you should use them as outer containers, and put your plant in its own pot down inside.

326

Two Essentials

Along with the various types of pots, there are a couple of other points to consider: the drainage hole, and the drip saucer.

Rule Number 1   Never—repeat, NEVER—put a plant in any kind of pot that does not have a drainage hole.

If you do, you are asking for trouble. And you will get it. If you overwater a plant, the excess water has no place to go; roots will sit in the water, and it doesn't take much of that before they rot. The plant's a goner.

On the other hand, if your soil is a good mixture that drains well, and if your pot has a hole, even if you overwater you won't do serious damage, because the water just runs out.

Which brings us to the next point. When that water runs out, where does it go? Onto your furniture, unless the pot has a saucer to catch the drips.

Rule Number 2   Make sure all pots have saucers.

The pot that the plant comes in from the store often does not have a saucer. You can add a separate saucer (buy them separately at the plant store or use an extra plate or pie pan from your kitchen cupboard), or you can slide the whole thing, pot and all, into another, larger pot that you chose for looks.

The purpose of the saucer is to protect your furniture or floor from spills and drips. Be aware that sometimes condensation forms on the bottom of a plastic saucer, so the furniture may be getting wet underneath the saucer. If you're putting a plant in a particularly precious spot, such as your grand piano or a family antique, add another layer of protection. You can buy saucers that have little feet, to let air circulate underneath; or rounds of cork that will absorb the condensation.

Saucers made of terra-cotta present an interesting conundrum: they catch drips from the pot, but they themselves drip. Like the clay pots, clay saucers are porous and will leak water through the pores. If the plant is in a sensitive spot, either apply a coat of waterproofing to the saucer or use a plastic liner.

Containers for Hanging Plants

Everything we've said about pots so far also applies to hanging containers. The plastic/clay trade-offs are the same; the warning about drainage holes and drip saucers still holds. In fact, that warning may be even more important with hanging baskets, because it's easy to forget to provide for drips.

Hanging baskets are very popular for plants that trail downward; it's the best way to display the cascading growth. They're not all literally baskets, but the term is often used to include all kinds of containers. In all cases, think carefully about where you'll put the hook. Hanging baskets can get surprisingly heavy; if your hook is in the ceiling, make sure it is anchored into a joist. For small pots, you can use a bracket that attaches to a wall or window frame and extends out from the wall.

About the simplest arrangement is a standard clay or plastic pot, along with its drip saucer, with a rope or chain sling that passes underneath the saucer and comes up around the pot to fasten to a hook at the top. An elegant variation of this system is a circle of steel wire with a round holder at the bottom of the circle that the saucer fits into.

To make your hanging container fancy, you can use any sort of decorative container; just put the regular pot, with a drainage hole, down inside it. You can use even use an actual basket, as long as you put something inside to catch the drips; either the saucer that comes with the pot, or something wide and shallow like a pie tin.

With hanging baskets, a couple of points you must keep in mind:

1. Be sure you can reach the plant to water it. If you have a wonderful cathedral ceiling and a plant way up there, you'll need some kind of pulley system to bring the plant down where you can reach it.
2. Up there near the ceiling, it's a few degrees warmer than down where you're standing. So the plant will need watering more often than if it were at floor level.
3. For the same reason, a humidity-loving plant will need

328

extra attention. Mist it more often, or pack sphagnum moss around the pot and keep the moss damp. Or both.

The wrong way. When you put a pot inside a decorative container, don't set it directly on the bottom. Water that collects there can lead to root rot.

Decorative Outer Containers

There are many beautiful things to put plants in: silver bowls, antique pots, intricately woven baskets, colorful pottery, family treasures, souvenirs of special vacations, all kinds of wonderful containers that have special meaning to you or harmonize with your room decor.

The right way. A layer of pebbles in a decorative outer pot will raise the inner pot up above the level of water, so roots don't sit in water.

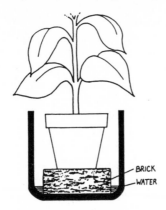

The right way. Another way to keep the plant up out of harm's way is to set it on a brick, as here, or a small block of wood.

But there's no drainage hole—can you use them? Sure. Just don't put the soil directly into the bottom. Use the special container as an outer decoration, and put your plant—in its own pot—down inside: a pot within a pot.

The right way. Special decorative containers can make any plant look spectacular, but be sure to provide a way to keep the pot up out of the drainage water. A layer of sphagnum moss can be added to hide the inner pot and to help provide humidity.

One word of caution: Don't set the pot on the bottom of the outer container (unless it has its own drip saucer). The water that runs out the drainage hole has nowhere to escape, and so it will sit in the bottom of your outer pot. It will wick back up through the drainage hole and into the soil, leaving the roots vulnerable to rot. The solution is to put something in the bottom to lift the pot up: a brick, a block of wood, an upside-down saucer or bowl, or a layer of gravel.

If there's a lot of space between the inner and outer pots, you can add sphagnum moss to fill in the gap. If the plant is one that likes humidity (and most houseplants do), keep the moss damp and you have created a mini-environment that stays humid.

Potting Soil and Soil Additives

The next big question you have to deal with when repotting is: what kind of soil goes into the pot?

Remember that the soil now in the present pot will be going into the new pot along with the plant; so you need only enough to fill the extra space in the bigger pot. If you're doing only one plant, you may find it simplest to buy a small bag of houseplant potting mix and just use that.

But if you have a collection of houseplants, and you check them all at the same time (which you probably will, because that's the easiest way), chances are you'll be repotting more than one plant. Pretty soon you'll decide it makes sense to mix up your own potting soil; you'll save money buying large bags of the various ingredients and creating your own mixture. Here are some of the ingredients you will see in the stores, along with some prices from my local garden center in Portland, Oregon.

Potting soil. Not the houseplant mix mentioned just above; this looks more like plain dirt, but it is soil with a lot of organic material that has been sterilized. Cost: A four-quart bag (which is about the size of a ten-pound bag of sugar) was $1.50; a one-cubic-foot bag (about thirty quarts) was $4.00.

This soil contains all the nutrients a plant needs, but it is what gardeners call "heavy," which means that when it is wet it compacts tightly. This is bad for houseplants in two ways: the soil stays too wet, presenting the danger of root rot, and it's so waterlogged there's not enough room for oxygen. Most houseplants need a lighter mix, one that drains well and is better aerated. To achieve that, you will use this potting soil as your base and add other things to lighten it up.

Perlite. This is one of the things you can add to potting soil to make it more porous and better draining. Perlite is volcanic rock that has been heated to very high temperatures, which sterilizes it and makes it porous, and then pulverized into tiny bits. It looks like tiny white pebbles; a large bag is surprisingly lightweight. Cost: four quarts, $1.50; one cubic foot, $4.00.

Vermiculite. This is another way to add lightness to potting soil. Vermiculite is mica that has been heated very high, which expands the crystals and creates minute pockets that will hold water in soil. It too is very light, but it will hold up to ten times its own weight in water. Cost: four quarts, $1.50; one cubic foot, $4.00.

You need either perlite or vermiculite, but not both. Perlite contains fluoride, which causes some plants to turn brown on the tips. However, it lasts longer. Vermiculite does not have the fluoride, but it breaks down more quickly in soil and gradually disappears.

Sphagnum moss. This moss is collected in boggy areas, dried, and packaged for sale. In the package it's green-brown and stringy looking; when you soak it in a pail of water, it will absorb twenty times its weight. It adds some nitrogen to the soil. It is relatively sterile and contains a natural fungicide, so it is a very good material for starting cuttings. In World War I it was used as gauze.

Peat moss. Sphagnum moss in much finer particles; it has been allowed to decompose naturally or been ground up. It is extremely lightweight, with a fine, powdery texture. It takes forever to get wet, but once it is wet, it holds water for a very long time. Cost: $1.50 for four quarts; $4.00 for one cubic foot.

Sphagnum moss and peat moss are added to houseplant mix in order to create soil that retains water; for moisture-loving plants, you would use one or the other.

Sand. Sand has the opposite effect—it makes water run through the soil quickly. Aside from improving drainage, it has no nutritional value. Don't use sand you dig at the beach; the salt will hurt the plants. Cost: A small bag of sand in the garden section of a big variety store cost me $1.29 (about five pounds). In the building supply section of the same store, an eighty-pound bag of builder's sand (washed river sand, same as the small bag) cost $3.19.

Charcoal. Have you ever smelled a wet burlap sack that's been in the trunk of your car for a few days? Your potting soil can take on that same sour smell after a while; a little pinch of charcoal will prevent the sour odor. It's not a necessity, but a small bag (one quart, $2.50) will last you a long time. Use charcoal meant for plants or aquariums, not for the barbecue grill.

Remember, you don't need *all* these things. To make your own mix, spread some newspapers on the floor and table. Find a large container to mix in and a smaller container, like an old juice pitcher, to use as a measure.

- Start with one unit of potting mix.
- Add one half unit of either perlite or vermiculite.
- Add a sprinkle of charcoal (optional).
- If you are repotting plants that like damp soil (such as ferns), add a half unit of sphagnum moss or peat moss to make the soil hold water better.
- If you're repotting cacti or succulents, add a half unit of sand, to make the soil drain faster.

The next time you're in the plant store, notice the special soil mixes available: for cacti, for African violets, for orchids, and probably for a lot more. They work fine, and are a wonderful shortcut.

Does Your Plant Need Repotting?

There are three ways to tell very quickly if your plant is ready for a new pot.

1. If roots are growing out of the drainage hole, that's an obvious distress signal.

If roots are growing out the drainage hole, the plant is trying to tell you something: it's time to repot.

2. The roots have completely filled the pot and are growing around in circles. How do you know? As part of your regular spring maintenance, slide the plant out of the pot (see directions below) and take a look at the roots. If you see mostly soil, with just a few root ends poking through, it's not time to repot yet; just slide the whole mass right back into the pot.

3. If when you add water to the plant, it *immediately* pours out of the drainage hole as fast as you pour it in, you have a problem. Either the soil has totally dried out, or the roots have so completely filled the pot that they are self-strangling and can't take up any water at all.

Once a year, slide all plants out of their pots. If the roots are growing around in circles like this, it's time to repot.

If you have the third situation, here's how to tell which of the two problems you're facing. If the soil is thoroughly dried out, it will have pulled away from the edge of the pot a little bit, so you can tell by looking. (The cure is to soak the whole

If roots have thoroughly filled the pot, any water you add will run right out as fast as you pour it in. If that happens to you, check the soil. If it's pulled away from the edges of the pot, as here, it has totally dried out. If the soil looks okay on the surface but won't take up any water, your plant is probably rootbound.

pot up to its rim in a bucket of water, and hold it there until the soil gradually gets wet.) If the soil isn't a tight, dried-up ball that has shrunk inside the pot, then you have the second problem, strangled roots; this can be verified by taking the plant out of the pot, as described below.

Not all plants need repotting annually. Many can go two or three years in the same pot, and some plants actually do better when they are moderately rootbound (this condition is known as being "tight in the pot"). Moderately rootbound means that the roots have reached the edge of the pot; if roots are growing around and around in a tight tangled mass, it's time for a move. The encyclopedia section of this book notes plants that do best when they are tight in their pots, and chapter 2 contains a list of plants that need repotting less often than average.

This adds up to a pretty simple rule of thumb:

When to Check a Plant's Roots

1. When you bring a new plant home.
2. Once a year after that.

How to Look at the Roots

1. Water the plant very thoroughly; the idea is to get the soil as loose as possible.
2. Slide your fingers around the base of the plant.
3. Turn the pot upside down and hit the top rim sharply against a countertop or a table; you're trying to loosen the root ball.
4. Keep holding the pot upside down, and the plant should slide out into your hand through gravity.
5. If not, push gently through the drainage hole with a pencil and pull the plant at the soil line ever so gently.
6. If that still doesn't work, slide a table knife all around the edge of the pot and try again.

Repotting Step by Step

Step 1. Prepare the New Pot

- The new pot should be one size larger than the present pot.
- If it's a new clay pot, submerge it (empty) in a sinkful of water till it's thoroughly wet.
- If the new pot has been used before, make sure it's clean. If it's plastic, wash in soapy water and then rinse. If it's clay, you'll have to wash and then sterilize it (soak it in a mild solution of household bleach) to get rid of insecticide and fertilizer residues.
- Add a shallow layer of small pebbles or gravel to the bottom.

Step 2. Get Your Potting Soil Ready

- Use houseplant mix straight from the bag, or mix your own, according to the guidelines above in the section on soils.
- Put a moderate amount of soil into the new pot; leave lots of room for the plant and its present soil.

To take a plant out it its pot, first water it thoroughly, then slide your hand around the base of the plant.

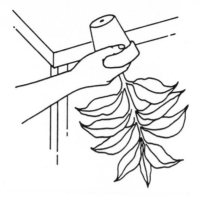

Knock the pot against the side of a table or counter, to loosen the soil from the edge of the pot.

Step 3. Take the Plant out of the Pot

- Using the technique described in "How to Look at the Roots" (illustrated here), slide the plant out of the old pot. Try to keep the soil ball intact.
- If the roots are tightly entwined, loosen them up with your fingers. Be gentle.

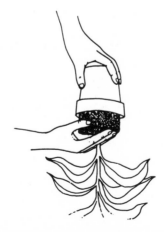

Hold the pot upside down and the plant should slide out into your other hand, soil and all.

After you have taken a rootbound plant out of its old pot, set the plant and its soil ball into the new pot, into which you have already put a layer of pebbles and an inch or so of new potting soil.

Step 4. Put the Plant in the New Pot

- Set the plant, with old soil intact, into the center of the new pot.
- Hold the plant steady with one hand, and with the other fill in all around with new soil. Leave about an inch of space at the top.

Fill in all around with new soil, gently pressing down; leave an inch clearance at the top.

Here's an alternate way to get the larger pot ready to receive a plant that is being transplanted. Add some potting soil, then press in a small pot as a mold.

- Shake the pot a few times to settle the soil. Gently firm the top layer.
- Water very thoroughly.

You may have noticed something missing in these instructions: adding a piece of broken crock to the bottom to cover up the drainage hole. "Crock" originally meant a piece of broken clay pot, but more broadly it means any small, flat stone large enough to cover up the hole.

When you take away the empty pot, you have a space just the right size to accommodate the plant and its existing soil ball.

This omission is deliberate: it is not a good idea to completely cover up this hole. It doesn't help drainage (as is commonly supposed); in fact it hinders it. What is worse, it removes an early warning sign of trouble. Roots growing out the bottom may be your first clue that your plant is rootbound; if that hole is blocked, they will grow into a serious contorted mass before they work their way under the stone and out through the hole. Besides, how many people have pieces of broken pots lying around?

Working with Large Plants

Checking the root system of very large plants is tricky. If the pot is so large you can't pick it up, you can't very well knock the plant out to take a look at the roots. You'll have to lay the plant on its side and get a friend to help you slide it out.

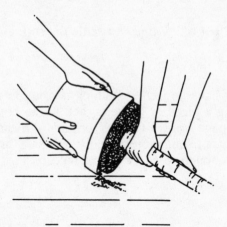

Taking a very large plant out of its pot is a two-person job.

If you discover that it's time to repot, but you don't have a larger pot and don't want the plant to grow any taller anyway, you have only one choice: trim the roots, put the whole thing back in the same pot, and add some fresh soil.

Root pruning takes a bit of courage. Common sense tells you it's not a good idea to take a knife and cut off roots. But the plant will survive. It will grow new roots to replace what

Root pruning will allow you to put a rootbound plant back into the same pot with some fresh soil; if the plant has already grown as big as you want, this is a way to control its size.

you cut off, yet will still fit in the same pot, which is what you're trying to accomplish.

Slide the whole root ball out of the pot. With a *very* sharp knife, slice down through the outer edge of the root system, trimming off slices until the root mass will fit back in the pot and leave about an inch to spare all around. Fill in with new soil, and water thoroughly.

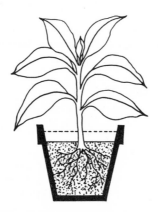

When a plant is too large to take out of its pot, you can give it fresh soil with a technique called top dressing. Remove about an inch of soil from the top.

Then replace with new soil, so the plant has a fresh supply of nutrients.

You probably won't need to repeat this operation for a few years, but next year you will want to give the plant new soil. The way to do that is a procedure called "top dressing." With a spoon or spatula, carefully remove the top layer of soil, about an inch down. Replace it with an equal amount of fresh soil. The plant gets the benefit of the nutrients in the new soil, and you don't have to wrestle that big plant out of its pot.

Repotting a Cactus
A cactus plant has a very shallow root system, and grows very slowly, so it will be long time before it gets so rootbound that it needs a larger pot. But when it does, you'll need extra care to get the plant moved without hurting yourself on the thorns.

One way is to wear heavy protective gloves. Another is to use a sling of folded newspaper or a towel, so that your hands never touch the plant.

Support Systems

Plants that are naturally climbers—monstera, philodendrons, ivy, and so on—will do much better if you give them something to hang on to. And repotting time is the time to do it.

Be careful when removing a spiny cactus from its pot. Wear heavy gloves, or make a protective sling from newspaper.

If you buy a very large plant, it may come with some kind of support pole. When you move the plant to a larger pot, check to see that the pole is still sturdy (they eventually rot at the soil line), and replace it if necessary.

But if you buy a small plant, it probably does not come with a support, and you should add one the first time you transplant to a larger pot. Prepare the new pot, put in the first layer of new soil, add the pole, then insert the plant last. To help it get started, tie the stem loosely to the pole in a couple of places.

You will find many kinds of support for sale at the garden center. There are small trellises made of wood or plastic. There are poles made of compressed wood fibers with a rough surface texture something like the bark of a tree. And for small plants a simple bamboo stake is hard to beat.

One item on the shelves that may be new to you is a moss stick: sphagnum moss compressed onto a wooden core. It is very effective as a support because plants with aerial roots find clinging to its rough texture very easy, and also because being moss it retains moisture, which the little roots are very happy for.

You can easily make a moss stick yourself. If you have access to chicken wire, make a cylinder out of wire, crimp the

A moss pole is an excellent support for a climbing vine like this philodendron. The moss retains moisture and provides a rough surface for the plant's aerial roots to grab. This one is rolled-up chicken wire, stuffed with sphagnum moss to retain moisture and a round dowel to give stability.

edges together, and pack it full of sphagnum moss (a broom handle is a good packing aid). Wet the moss well, and bury the whole thing in the pot. To make things even stronger, first put a round dowel inside the wire cylinder and pack moss all around it; the dowel helps the moss pole stand more firmly in

To help your plant get established on a moss pole, pin the stems at a few places with hairpins.

the pot. Then add the plant, and help it get started by pinning the bottom stems to the pole with bent wire or old-fashioned hairpins.

The chicken wire is effective because the wire crosspieces give the plant something easy to grab on to. But you can make a perfectly acceptable pole without wire. Start with a tall stick or dowel and a bag of sphagnum moss. Wet the moss well and then simply tie it on with string or wire; leave the bottom of the stick bare, so it's easier to insert in the soil, and you're done.

All moss sticks, either store-bought or homemade, should be kept damp; that encourages the roots. Keep your spray bottle handy, and spray the pole when it looks dry.

Repotting Checklist

√ Check every new plant as soon as you get it home; slide it out of the pot and examine the root ball. After that, check them all once a year; spring is a good time.

√ Best time to repot is early in the spring; the plant is about to start a new spurt of growth and will quickly recover from the shock then.

√ Considering a pot without a drainage hole? Put it back.

√ Don't use soil that you dig up out of the backyard; it's full of weed seeds, insect larvae, and other yucky stuff.

7

🍒 🍒 🍒

The Nursery:
Making Baby Plants

You won't have houseplants for long before you get interested in propagation—making baby plants from parts of mature plants. The first time you trim off an end of your wandering jew because you know it needs shaping and then decide to root the cut part instead of throwing it away, you've started propagating. And you're hooked. It's one of the most satisfying aspects of enjoying houseplants.

There are several ways to propagate plants, and most of them are easy.

Stem Cuttings

Plants with Soft Stems
This is the technique you will be using the most, partly because it's the easiest and partly because stem cuttings come into your life whether you want them or not. If you have any plant that grows as a vine—philodendron, wandering jew, syngonium—you need to keep cutting it back so it maintains a nice full shape. And the part you trim off is a natural for a stem cutting.

But for purposes of explanation, let's assume you're making

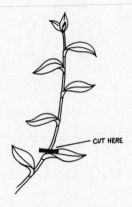

To make a new plant, cut off an end of wandering jew just above a leaf.

a cutting specifically for propagation. The basic procedure has four steps.

1. Your cutting should have at least four healthy leaves. Choose a point on the parent plant just above a node—that slightly thick place on the stem where a leaf (or set of leaves) is attached. Cut with scissors or a sharp knife, unless the stem is so soft that you can pinch it off with your fingers.

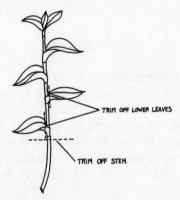

Trim off and discard the bottom part of the stem, where there are no leaves, and then remove the lower leaves.

2. Trim off the lowest part of the stem, between the cut end and the next node, and throw that segment away. Now trim away the lowest one or two leaves, all the way back to the stem. You should have at least two leaves left; three is better. At this point you can dip the end in rooting hormone, but that is optional.
3. Put the cutting in a glass of water. In a couple of weeks, roots will begin to form; they grow out of the nodes, where the lower leaves were.

Place the cutting in a glass of water. Roots will develop where the lower leaves were.

4. When there is a good healthy-looking mass of roots, take the cutting out of the water and plant it in a pot. Now you've got a new plant, for yourself or a gift.

Rooting cuttings in water is the most popular method, because it's so easy and because you can easily see when the roots have formed. But you can use other materials too. Any of the soil additives described in chapter 6 (perlite, vermiculite, sphagnum moss, or sand) work fine, as long as you keep them damp.

The cutting does not need the nutrients in soil in order to form roots; it will use the energy stored in the nodes. It needs

Cuttings can also be rooted in solid material, as well as water. You can use sand, vermiculite, perlite, peat moss, or any combination of these. Dampen your material, and make a hole for the stem.

water (or some other damp substance) to keep from wilting while the roots are growing. So it doesn't really matter what the cutting is sitting in, or standing in, as long as it stays moist.

You can also put a cutting directly into a small pot filled with regular potting mix, and root it there. The advantage is

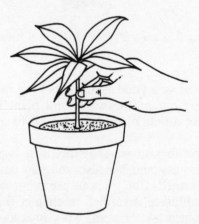

Add the cutting, firming the soil around the stem. In a larger pot, you can root several cuttings at once.

that it can just stay in that pot; you won't have to replant it. The disadvantage is that you cannot tell by looking whether roots have formed. (After two weeks, tug gently; if the cutting doesn't lift out easily, it has rooted.)

Tie a clear plastic bag around the pot to make a mini-greenhouse; your cutting will root faster this way. Be careful: if it is too damp the stem will rot before the roots form.

Plants with Hard Stems

Plants that have tough, woody stems are somewhat more difficult to propagate. If they have branches, you can take a cutting from the end of a branch, and follow the same steps as for soft-stem cuttings above. There is one extra step.

Plants with hard stems root more slowly than those with soft stems. You can encourage the process by using rooting hormone. The hormone is in the form of a powder; pour a small amount into a dish and coat the end of the cutting.

If the plant you want to propagate has only one main stem, like a tree, the only way you can make a stem cutting is to cut the top off the plant. Perhaps you want to do that anyway, if the plant has lost its lower leaves and now looks badly unbalanced. (Review the pruning section of chapter 4.) If all goes well, you can get three separate plants from one.

The basic steps are these:

Plant No. 1

1. Coming down from the top of the plant, decide how much stem is needed to go with the leaves. Cut off the top section at that point.
2. Dip the cut end in rooting hormone.
3. Plant in sterile rooting material like peat moss; keep it damp and warm. Rooting can take weeks.

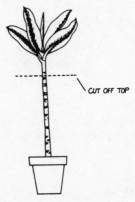

CUT OFF TOP

You may be able to get several plants from one tall plant with a single woody stem. Start by cutting off top segment. Dip the cut end in rooting hormone and root in damp soil or sand. That's plant number 1.

Plant No. 2

1. Coming up from the soil line, decide where you would like new leaves to sprout. Cut there, using a sharp knife or pruning shears.
2. Now you have a bare stick coming up from the pot, with no leaves. Keep the soil moist, and keep your fingers crossed. Many plants will put out new growth from the energy stored in the stem and roots. Even if this part dies, you're still ahead.

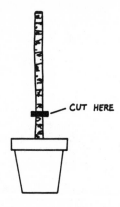

For plant number 2, cut off the bare stem at the point where you want new leaves the sprout; keep the soil damp. This is a lengthy process.

Plant No. 3

1. Now you should have a separate section of stem with at least one node. If your length of stem is long enough to have several nodes, cut it into pieces; each piece should have at least one node.
2. Prepare damp rooting material—moss, sand, vermiculite, whatever. A glass of water doesn't work too well here.

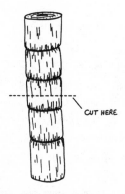

From the bare stem that remains, you can get one or more additional plants. Start by cutting the stem section into pieces with at least one node each; those shown here have two nodes apiece.

Each piece of stem goes in damp sand, either horizontally or vertically. Make sure a node is in contact with the sand.

3. Place the cutting into the rooting material either horizontally or vertically. If vertical, make sure that one node is underground. If horizontal, make sure the whole thing is halfway buried.
4. Keep the rooting material damp. Roots will form from the underground nodes, and leaves will sprout from the nodes that are aboveground. Be patient; this takes a while.

Roots will form where the underground nodes are; leaves will sprout from the nodes up above the soil.

Another propagation method that is appropriate for a tall-stemmed plant is air layering, which is described below.

Leaf Cuttings

Many plants will make babies from individual leaves. This is called, as you might imagine, a leaf cutting, and it is the standard way of propagating African violets. The technique is described and illustrated in chapter 3, under *Saintpaulia*.

A number of succulents propagate easily with leaf cuttings. In fact, they'll do this on their own, without any help from you. Leaves drop from the mother plant, land in the soil, and take root there; eventually tiny plants develop from the stem end of the leaf. You can lift these babies out, if you wish, and transplant them into their own small pots.

A Special Container for Cuttings

Many cuttings will root in a plain old glass of water, and it could be that's all you'll ever need. But you may not want lots of glasses sitting around on your windowsill. To speed the process along, and to keep all your cuttings in one place where you can keep an eye on them, you might want to use a propagation box.

A prop box, to use its nickname, is useful for leaf and stem cuttings, both soft and hard stems. You can make one from any container that has a removable top and is transparent enough to let light through. It doesn't have to be fancy—an old plastic shoebox is perfect. Or you can rig up a box using a clear plastic cake cover on top of a casserole dish.

The idea is that the cover lets light in and keeps moisture and heat from escaping. It's a miniature greenhouse, and things will happen quickly. Cuttings will root more quickly than if exposed to the open air—and fungus and rot will develop more quickly too.

Fill your prop box with solid rooting material—perlite, peat moss, vermiculite, sand, or any mixture of these; don't use regular potting soil, because it may not be completely sterile. Dampen the material first, then spread in a layer about one-fourth to one-third the depth of the container; leave enough room for the cuttings.

Use a pencil or chopstick to poke small holes in the stuff in the box and insert the cuttings, making sure at least one node is underground. Cover the box, and you're done.

Check every few days that it's not too moist (if the cover is steamed up all the time, it's too wet) or too dry (lift off the cover and test the soil with your finger). If you see mold or the stems are rotted from excess moisture, throw everything out and start over.

In a week, grasp a cutting at the soil line and pull slightly; if it comes right up, it's not rooted. If there's resistance, it's probably ready. Using a spoon or fork, lift the cutting out along with a clump of soil and verify that roots have formed. If so, congratulations—you have a new plant, ready to be transferred to its own pot of regular potting mix.

Air Layering

If you have a tall, single-stemmed plant like a dracaena, rubber plant, or dieffenbachia, and it has a long stretch of ugly bare stem, you have two choices. You can lop off the top and root

Another way to deal with a plant that has too much trunk is the technique called air layering. It is similar to making a stem cutting except that you don't cut the top all the way off.

it separately, as described above in the section on stem cuttings of hard-stemmed plants. That top section will *probably* root, and the bare stem remaining in the pot *may* send out new leaves as well.

Or you can try air layering, which is a way to root a segment of stem while it still attached to the main plant. In broad terms, here's how it works. You cause roots to develop at some point on the stem, then remove that rooted section and pot the plant; you have a new plant, with healthy roots and a stem that's the right length. (With the remaining stem, you can make stem cuttings.) With air layering you're more assured of success, because the plant is still alive while the operation is going on, but some people think it is unattractive. That's one of life's trade-offs.

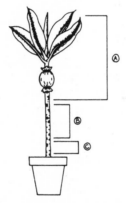

This rubber plant is being air layered. The top section, A, will eventually be a separate plant. The middle section of stem, B, can be turned into stem cuttings. And the bottom section, C, will sprout new leaves if the soil is kept damp. All told, at least three plants from one.

Step by step, here's how it works.

1. Decide how much stem you want for the new plant. Look at the leaves; how much stem do you need to go with them to make a balanced plant? Mark that spot.

2. At or near the node that is closest to your mark, make a cut *halfway* through the stem, angling upward. Use a sharp knife.

The first step in air layering is to cut *partway* through the stem, near a node; this is where the new roots will form. Use a match to keep the cut open.

3. Slide a wooden matchstick up into the cut, sideways. You want the cut to stay open, rather than healing itself, because this is where the roots will form.

4. Take several handfuls of wet sphagnum moss and wrap

Then tie a bundle of wet sphagnum moss all around the cut.

Now tie clear plastic around the whole thing. The plastic will hold in moisture, and will allow you to watch the progress.

them all around the cut area. Tie the moss in place with twine.
5. Take a piece of strong clear plastic and cover the moss; tie tightly above and below, making an airtight cocoon all around the moss.

CUT HERE

When you can see roots growing through the moss, your new plant is ready. Remove the plastic, cut through the stem below the roots, and plant this portion in its own pot.

360

6. It will take time, maybe as much as two months, but eventually roots will begin to develop. When you can see them growing through the moss (and that's why you used clear plastic), you're ready.
7. Undo the plastic and remove the moss. With knife or pruning shears, cut all the way through the stem, just below the new roots. You have a complete plant: roots, stem, and leaves. Transplant it into its own pot.
8. Now you can cut segments of the remaining stem, and root them as stem cuttings (see above). And if you keep the soil in the original pot damp, you may be rewarded with new leaves sprouting there too.

Division

Another technique that is good to have in your repertoire is known as division. It means cutting, or pulling, the entire plant—leaves, stems, and roots—into two or more pieces, each of which then gets repotted and grows into a full plant on its own. Instead of one overcrowded plant, you now have two or more.

Plants that send up stems from a central point are best propagated by division. Using your hands, pull the root ball apart into two or more segments. Now you have two plants instead of one overcrowded one.

It's the only way you can propagate some kinds of plants, principally those whose leaves grow straight from the soil without branching, such as aspidistra, spathiphyllum, and most ferns.

You could also use division if your plant has outgrown its pot but you want to keep it in that pot. Divide the plant into two; one half can go back in the pot you like; the other goes into another pot.

The technique is not hard, but it does take courage the first time you do it.

1. Take the entire plant out of its pot (see repotting directions in chapter 6). Put the plant on a work surface that you have covered with plastic or newspapers.
2. Examine the plant carefully at the soil line; you're looking for the best place to divide. Some plants send up leaf stems from a central cluster; if you can see where one cluster ends and another one begins, that's a natural dividing place.
3. Try pulling the plant apart. If it separates easily, pull it into sections with your hands. But don't force it, or you'll damage the roots. If there's any serious resistance, use a sharp knife and cut down through the root ball.

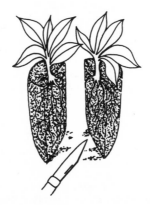

If roots won't separate easily, you'll need a sharp knife to divide. Pot each part separately, and new growth will quickly fill in to soften the sharp edge.

4. Plant each section separately in its own pot. If you had to use a knife, one side will look obviously cut for a while, but the plant will quickly fill in.

Offsets

Some plants reproduce themselves by sending out short underground stems from which a baby plant grows; the babies are called offsets. They are usually nestled in tight against the mother, and are exact miniatures, easily recognized as new plants. Some of the plants that produce offsets are the bromeliads and the low-growing succulents (see *Echeveria* in chapter 3).

In the wild, the mother plant and the baby would share the same spot for a long time; eventually the mother would die off (although it's a lengthy process) and the baby would grow to full size, someday producing its own offset. When we have them as houseplants, we don't have to wait for this full cycle. We can cut off the offset and plant it on its own.

CUT HERE

The way to propagate plants that produce offsets is to cut off the offset and pot it separately. The horizontal stem is usually underground; when you have a fully developed baby, cut right down through the soil with a sharp knife. Notice that a third plant is starting to develop from a node to the right of the mother. When it is bigger, it can be separated too.

Many of the succulents that produce offsets will eventually have a cluster of perfectly formed little plants surrounding the mother. It is a charming look, and you may want to leave the babies in place.

With bromeliads, however, don't wait too long. A bromeliad offset is growing underneath the mother's foliage, which is quite stiff; the baby will not develop an upright, balanced shape unless it is separated from its mother. Once it produces an offset, a bromeliad has begun to die. The process can take a year, and you may want to remove the offset and enjoy the colorful foliage of the mother plant for as long as possible. Or simply cut away the mother plant and let the baby develop in that same pot.

8

🍒 🍒 🍒

Terrariums and
Dish Gardens

In another chapter of this book you read one absolute, un-breakable rule: never put a plant in a container that has no drainage hole. Well, there is one exception.

Terrariums and dish gardens are unique ways of displaying plants; they create a mini-environment that is just right for certain plants at the same time that they create a piece of living art to highlight the decor of a room. And they are made from containers that don't have holes.

Strictly speaking, a terrarium is an all-glass plant container that has a top so that no water vapor escapes. We will use a definition that is a bit looser: a glass container that at least partially encloses the plant; it may or may not have a top. Glass containers that are open at the top are called "open terrariums" in this book.

A dish garden is a miniature landscape, made by planting several compatible plants in a shallow container; the container could be glass but usually isn't, and it doesn't have the high sides that hold in moisture.

Terrariums

How Does a Terrarium Work?
First of all, remember that plants give off water vapor through their leaves, as part of the natural life cycle. Water vapor is

water—H_2O—in the form of a gas. In a normal setting, that water vapor from the leaves is dispersed into the atmosphere around the plant. But in a covered terrarium, the water vapor has nowhere to go; it can't get out.

When it hits the sides of the glass, which have probably been warmed by the sunlight, the water vapor condenses into drops of water that eventually dribble down into the soil, through the force of gravity. The plant takes up the water from the soil through its roots, transpires it through the leaves as water vapor, and the cycle repeats.

When you plant a terrarium you add a little water to get things started. After a while, if all goes well, the plants settle into their protected environment and continually reuse the same water. Sometimes you'll see the sides of the container fogging up with steam and tiny drops of water, then things clear up again. If you chose a good location with the appropriate amount of light and planted correctly, theoretically the plants will live forever, or until they outgrow the container, whichever comes first.

Open terrariums do not fully contain the water vapor, but because they partially enclose the plant, they retain moisture and humidity more than regular pots do. You can think of them as being midway between a closed terrarium and a regular pot.

What Kind of Container?

For a true terrarium, any container with glass sides and a top will work. Some possibilities with ready-made tops are wide-mouth fruit jars, glass canisters, apothecary jars, and old-fashioned "general store" round jars with the opening on the side. Browse through any kitchen shop, hardware store, or department store, and you will see many familiar objects that can be turned into successful terrariums. Just be sure you choose something that has an opening large enough to get your hand in.

Open terrariums present even more possibilities: large brandy snifters, bowls, aquarium tanks, fishbowls, antique pitchers, just about any attractive container that is made of glass and is large enough to hold a plant or two.

Terrariums can be planted in a wide variety of glass containers, both with and without tops.

And of course if you add a top to an open terrarium you have a closed terrarium. You can get a glass shop to cut a circle of glass just the right size; Plexiglas works too, and so does plastic food wrap, although it is less attractive.

The one container that you will want to avoid is a bottle or jug with a skinny neck. You may see pictures of terrariums planted in wine bottles, especially the kind with fat round bottoms, along with "simple" directions for how they were done.

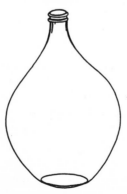

But don't try planting a terrarium in something with a very small neck. It's very difficult, and the results are almost always disappointing.

The truth is, it's very difficult. It's hard to get the plants positioned firmly, it's hard to keep from getting dirt on the sides and very hard to clean it up when you do, and it's practically impossible to get down in there to do any kind of maintenance on the plants. So if a leaf dies off (which it will), it will lie on the soil and rot, looking ugly and breeding disease. Bottle terrariums are not worth the trouble.

The container can be either clear glass, which gives you the most flexibility in choosing plants, or lightly tinted, in which case you will have the best success if you plant only shade-loving plants.

How About the Soil?

The basic potting mix for a terrarium is the same as for "normal" pots; review chapter 6. You will probably want to add some moisture-retaining peat moss, and you need something to keep the soil well aerated: either perlite or vermiculite.

The part about terrariums that's different is that you have to add a drainage layer. You always want to avoid having the roots of the plants sit in water. Since there is no hole for any excess water to escape through, you must add a protective layer on the very bottom; extra water can collect there, but the roots never reach it.

This layer can be pebbles, crushed rock, pieces of broken clay pots. Keep in mind that because the container is glass, this layer is as visible as the plants, and so make it as attractive as you can. Clear or colored glass marbles, for example, are more expensive than rocks, but you may decide their special effect is worth the extra cost.

The drainage layer goes in first; it should be as deep as the soil layer is going to be, at least an inch. Next, spread a layer of wet sphagnum moss on top of the drainage rocks so that soil cannot dribble down through it.

Then lay down a thin layer of charcoal pieces, one pebble deep; the charcoal will dispel any sour odor that develops. This is more important in a terrarium than in an open pot, for the buildup of unpleasant aroma will be very noticeable in a closed environment.

Now add the soil. Moisten it first, just till it is very lightly damp through and through. Put in enough to hold the plants. Together the soil plus the drainage layer should take up about one fourth of the whole container.

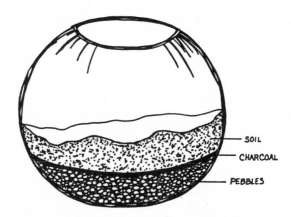

In a terrarium, which has no drainage hole, it is crucial that you provide a substantial drainage layer. Here about an inch of pebbles will allow any excess water to settle to the bottom, safely away from the plants' roots. A bit of charcoal prevents a sour smell.

Choosing the Plants

Remember that the terrarium is an intensely concentrated environment; all the plants will share the same circumstances, so you should select plants that have very similar needs.

For closed terrariums choose plants that need high humidity, moist soil, and constant temperature. Then, depending on where you plan to put your terrarium, they should all be low-light or medium-light plants. Check the lists in chapter 2.

For open terrariums, the list is longer, since you can select plants that don't need the superhigh humidity levels. You can also use the same plants as for closed terrariums, as long as you keep an eye on the water level.

Plants for Terrariums

Any of the pileas
Any of the peperomias

Codiaeum variegatum
Fittonia
Dracaena godseffiana
Podocarpus macrophyllus
Hedera helix
Small ferns, especially *Adiantum, Asplenium,* and *Pteris*
Maranta
Iresine
Tolmiea menziesii
Saintpaulia

The following are also good while they are still baby plants; they will eventually need pruning or replacing.

> *Aglaonema*
> *Chamaedorea elegans*
> *Dizygotheca elegantissima*
> *Setcreasea*
> *Syngonium*
> *Tradescantia*
> *Zebrina*

For the most attractive arrangement, select an assortment of plants—varied leaf shape and colorations, some taller than others. Start with very small plants; that way, you'll have the fun of watching them grow and won't have to replace them for a while. If you can find miniature varieties, so much the better.

Decorating Tip

Open terrariums are a very beautiful way to display individual plants that you are especially proud of; it's like putting them on a pedestal with a spotlight on them. One stunning African violet in a brandy snifter, or a perfectly round bird's nest fern all by itself in a beautiful round bowl, is a lovely sight.

Planting and Maintaining the Terrarium

First decide where the finished terrarium will be kept; most need medium light but not a direct blast of sun. In that position, is it likely to be viewed from all sides, or will it have a definite "front" side?

Fill the container with the drainage layer and the damp soil. You may want to arrange the soil into small hills and valleys, especially if there is not much difference in the height of the plants you're using.

Form the soil into small valleys, and add your plants. Choose plants that have similar requirements for light, water, and humidity. A layer of moss here gives a woodsy look to the finished arrangement. If you start with very young plants, as here, you won't have to replace them for a while.

Before you start planting, decide on the final arrangement. Move the plants around, still in their original pots, until you find a grouping that looks balanced and fits the container. Then begin planting, starting with the tallest plant or the one in the middle, if your container is round.

Now spray all the plants with a fine spray and put the top on, if there is a top. In a few days a closed terrarium should show signs of water beading and collecting on the glass. If this "fog" goes away in a day or two, all is well; if it stays on the glass for more than a couple of days, there is too much moisture—leave the top off for a day.

An open terrarium won't have the fogged-up sides to show you how much water is in the system, but by the same token soil moisture is easy to check in an open terrarium: just stick your finger down into the soil. If it's really dry, add water.

And that's about it. Watch for dead and dying leaves, and remove them. If the plants grow too big, snip them back or take them out altogether. Keep an eye out for signs of mold or stem rot; about the only trouble you have with terrariums is too much moisture.

Dish Gardens

A dish garden is any group of plants planted into a shallow container. That means that the plants should have shallow root systems, or be slow growers, or both. Plants that fit this description perfectly are cacti, and that is why the most common kind of dish garden is a cactus garden. You may prefer to feature some of the many fascinating succulents, or to make a mixed garden.

SANDY SOIL MIX
CHARCOAL
PEBBLES

A dish garden for cacti or succulents must begin with a good solid layer for drainage. These plants are easily damaged if they sit in too-wet soil. Any excess water will drain down through the sandy soil and collect on the bottom, well away from the plants. Charcoal keeps the soil smelling "sweet."

Container and Soil

Any wide, shallow container will work. It can be round, square, oval, whatever, and it can be any material that you like: plastic, ceramic, clay, glass, metal. A large drip saucer for a clay pot is an excellent choice; terra-cotta and cacti seem to go together. In florist shops and garden centers you will find an assortment of shallow bowls made for bonsai plantings; they are usually made of glazed ceramic and are quite handsome.

The soil layers will be essentially the same as in terrariums, except that you have less room to work with, so each layer is thinner. Start with a drainage layer, then charcoal, then your potting mix.

You can buy premixed potting soil made especially for cactus, and if this is your only cactus planting it's probably a good idea. Or you can mix your own: start with basic potting mix and add an equal measure of sand. It is *very* important that the soil mixture provide for fast drainage; in such a shallow container, with no drainage hole, there is little room for error.

Planting and Maintaining Your Dish Garden

The first time you visit a plant store that has lots of cacti and succulents, you will be amazed at the variety of interesting shapes. It won't be easy to narrow your selection.

After you choose the plants you like, decide how you will arrange them.

It's a good idea to take the container along with you; then you'll know how many plants to buy, and what sizes. If you're including succulents, stick to the low-growing varieties like *Echeveria elegans.*

Back at home, experiment with various combinations; put the plants, still in their pots, inside the container and move them around until you get an arrangement you like.

Then put in your drainage layer and charcoal, and *very* lightly damp soil, and start planting. One at a time, remove the cacti from their pots. Wear thick leather gloves, or use a sling made of newspaper (see chapter 6). Make a little valley in the soil, and set the plant down in. Push the soil firmly around, and then move on to the next plant.

This desert garden features *Aloe aristata*, a small *Mammillaria*, and two bishop's caps, *Astrophytum myriostigma*. Three pretty stones add to the effect.

To finish off your arrangement, you might want to "pave" the soil around the plants with colorful rock chips, or add a few pretty rocks. And for a real conversation piece, make one dish garden of rocks and the very unusual succulent plant called "living stone."

You'll need to find a spot in the sun for your garden; cactus plants need bright light. Think about traffic patterns; if any of your plants have thorns, don't put the garden in a place where people are likely to brush against it.

Maintaining the dish garden is mostly a matter of careful watering. If your cacti suddenly start growing tall and stretched out, you've overwatered. Cut back immediately, and you may be able to save them.

9

❦ ❦ ❦

Answers to the
Most Common Houseplant
Questions

Q: Is it true that talking to your plants helps them grow better?

A: Not in any literal way. Some people say that the plants like the carbon dioxide we breathe on them, but they get that from the general atmosphere whether or not we're hovering over them. What really happens is that while you're talking to your plants, you're looking at them carefully so you're likely to spot any signs of trouble early.

Q: What about playing classical music for them?

A: Play whatever kind of music makes you happy. The plants don't care.

Q: How often should I water my plants?

A: You're not going to like this answer: "Whenever they need it." It just isn't possible to make a hard-and-fast rule, because there are so many variables. To begin with, different species of plants need vastly different amounts of water. And even the same plant will need different amounts depending on the time of year, the amount of sunlight, the temperature of the room, the kind of pot it's in, how big its root system is, and so on.

There's only one way to tell: stick your finger down into the soil an inch or so. If you don't like getting your hands dirty, you don't have much future as a gardener.

Q: My plant has yellow leaves on it. What that does mean?

A: Another answer you won't like: "It depends." Yellow leaves are a symptom of several different kinds of problems, some exact opposites of each other. Spend some time reviewing the information in chapter 5, and spend some time searching your heart about what you're doing to your plant.

Q: My plant looks very sick. What should I do?

A: First, move it to another location, away from other plants, so they don't get infected. Then look the plant over from top to bottom. Then read about the plant in the encyclopedia section. Then check the descriptions of symptoms in chapter 5.

Now start putting pieces together. Compare what you see with what you know you have been doing for your plant; compare what you have been doing with what the plant wanted you to do.

It's a process of elimination. When you have determined the most likely problem, you'll know what to do as a cure. If the signs are consistent with overwatering, and you just read that this plant needs to go mostly dry between waterings, and you know you watered it more than that, then the solution is clear: cut down on your watering schedule.

If the problem is a disease or insect infestation, follow the various techniques described in chapter 5. If it's bad, you may not be able to save the plant, but at least you can keep others from getting infected.

Q: What is "crock," and what do you do with it?

A: Originally it meant a piece of broken clay pot, and it was put in the bottom of a pot, with its convex side facing up, to form a barrier over the hole. Then the term was expanded to mean any kind of pebble put over the hole.

Q: What's it used for?

A: The usual answer is "to improve drainage"—but that's an old idea that should be buried. Experiments have proved that having a rock in the bottom of your pot does not improve drainage, it makes it worse.

And there is another reason not to do it: One of the ways you tell when your plant is rootbound is by having the roots grow out through the hole. If the hole is blocked, the roots will grow into a big mess before they find their way down under the rock, and you won't see the trouble in time.

Q: What if I don't have any potting mix? Can I use dirt from the yard?

A: Yes, but you'll have to sterilize it first, to kill weed seeds and insect larvae. Spread it on a cookie sheet, sprinkle water on it, and bake it in a 200-degree oven for two hours. Be prepared: it stinks.

Q: Should I put leaf shine on my plants?

A: No. It will just block the pores. Regularly wash the leaves with soapy water, and rinse; they'll shine on their own.

Q: Is there any plant I can put in the stairwell, where there are no windows at all?

A: Pick a plant from the low-light list in chapter 2; one week a month, give it a "vacation" in a well-lit room.

Q: What should I do with my plants while I'm on vacation?

A: If you're only going to be gone a week, you don't have a problem. Practically anything can go a week without water. Move everything except cacti away from the window; plants need more water in direct sunlight. If your trip is longer than a week, use one of these techniques:

- Water the plant well and cover with a clear plastic bag. Use chopsticks to keep the plastic up off the leaves. For very large plants, you can just cover the pot and soil; slide the bag up from underneath and tie it around the base of the plant, at the soil line.
- Fill your bathtub with plants, water them thoroughly, then stretch a sheet of plastic over the top of the tub and anchor it with tape. Put in a few tall stakes to keep the tops of plants from hitting the plastic, if necessary.

To water plants continuously while you're on vacation, rig up a wicking system. Thin strips of absorbent material wick water from the glass jar to both pots.

- Rig up a temporary wick watering system. Put one end of a strip of cotton fabric down into the soil, the other end in a bowl of water. You can do several plants together.
- Line a large cardboard box with plastic and pack it half full with wet sphagnum moss or sand. Put the plants in and tuck the moss around the pots. (This works best for plants in clay pots.)

Q: How can I tell if I'm buying a healthy plant?

A: You get a gold star for such a good question. First, in the store step back and look at all the plants. Do you get a general impression of vigor, health, lots of lush green foliage? That means the store has taken good care of its plants or they just got in a new shipment from the greenhouse. Either way, you have reason to feel confident; choose the individual plant you like, and check it for the following points.

- Are roots growing out the bottom? It's not fatal, but you know you'll have to repot almost at once.
- Look on the stem and underneath a few leaves for signs of insects.
- Pass up any plant that has had all its tips trimmed with scissors; it has been through some kind of stress that turned the tips brown, and someone has tried to remove the evidence.
- Poke the stem with your finger, right at the soil line; if it's mushy or soggy, it's probably rotting. Put it back.

If your first impression is of a mix of healthy and not-so-healthy plants, you'll have to examine individual plants even more carefully.

Q: What should I do when I get home with the new plant?
A: Flush the soil, to get rid of fertilizer buildup (greenhouses fertilize heavily, so that the merchandise grows fast). Do that by placing the plant in the kitchen sink and letting lots of water run through. If possible, keep the plant by itself for two weeks before you introduce it to your others. Don't put it in direct sun immediately, even if the plant can take bright light; start in a semi-shady spot and gradually move it to brightness. Don't panic if some leaves drop; it's a natural reaction to the stress of suddenly being in a new environment.

Q: Is air-conditioning bad for plants?
A: Not in itself, unless it is blasting a cold wind directly at a plant. If the air conditioner keeps the room at a temperature that is comfortable for you, chances are the

plants like that temperature too. Many plants like a room that is cool; most will tolerate it. The problem with air-conditioning is that it also dehumidifies a room, and low humidity *is* bad for most plants. You can solve the problem by misting more often or adding pebble trays (see chapter 4). Or if the air-conditioning is in your office, talk to your manager about adding a humidifier; it's good for people as well as plants.

Q: What is that white crud on the outside of my pots?

A: Presumably you mean clay pots. It's the residue of fertilizer that you have applied by dissolving it in water and applying to your soil. The plant's roots extract the nutrients in liquid form and some solid matter is left. Because the pot is porous, eventually these residues (they are called "fertilizer salts") work their way to the outside surface. It doesn't necessarily mean you've been over-fertilizing, but it should cause you to stop and consider the question.

To get rid of the crud, first flush the pot (put it in the sink and let *lots* of water run through), then scrub off the salts with a brush or pot scrubber.

These salts form in plastic pots, too, but you don't see them because they stay in the soil (plastic is not porous). To get rid of any buildup, flush the plant once a year.

Q: What is that green, mossy-looking crust on the top of the soil?

A: Moss. It forms in a too-moist environment. At some point, someone was overwatering this plant, and moss started to grow; then conditions were improved so it dried up. It's not serious, but you should remove it, because it can make the soil stiff so water doesn't penetrate well. Scrape it off with a spoon and remove the debris. Replace with an equal amount of new soil.

Q: Okay, I give up. What does *Nautilocalyx forgetii* mean?

A: Darned if I know. *Nautilo* means "like a ship," and the calyx is the base part of a flower. So the genus name means something like "with a calyx resembling a ship." But *forgetii*? Could it mean that someone forgot the name? Or forgot the plant? Or . . . ?

Glossary

Bract. A particular kind of a leaf that encloses a flower; it is usually brightly colored, and often mistaken for part of the flower. The red "flowers" of a poinsettia, for example, are bracts; the true flowers of poinsettia are those tiny white things inside the red "petals."

Cultivar. A man-made subspecies; a commercial variety developed in a greenhouse. The word comes from **culti**vated **vari**ety. Because it was intentionally developed, a cultivar is technically different from a variety, which is a subspecies that develops in nature. In a botanical name the cultivar is the third part of the name, and it is usually in quotation marks. An example is: *Cissus rhombifolia* 'Ellen Danika'.

Cutting. A piece of a plant that is deliberately removed, cut off, for the purpose of growing a new plant. Some people call a cutting a "slip."

Epiphytic. Growing in air. An epiphyte is a plant whose roots are exposed to air, rather than growing down in the soil. It takes in moisture and nutrients from the air and plant debris that collects around the roots. Often epiphytes attach themselves to branches of trees, but that is a mechanical convenience; they just use the tree as an anchor, and hang on by their toenails, as it were. They are not parasites on the tree; in fact, they could as easily attach themselves to a telephone wire—and sometimes do. The opposite of epiphytic is terrestrial, growing in the earth.

Family. In the classification system, family is the next category up from genus; one family can contain many genera.

Frond. The leaves of ferns are called fronds; usually they have long center ribs with many individual leaflets attached on both sides.

Genus. In the classification system, genus is the second to the bottom category. In one genus are grouped all the species that share certain characteristics; sometimes the traits that define a genus are invisible, such as certain ways the seed is shaped. The plural form of genus is *genera.*

Native. We say a plant is native to a certain area if it grows there naturally, without any interference from human beings present or past. Many plants were introduced into an area from somewhere else a very long time ago, so long that we tend to think they always grew there. But a plant is not a true native unless it originally grew there spontaneously.

Node. The slightly thicker point on the stem where all the growing energy is concentrated. Leaves develop from nodes, and cuttings develop roots at nodes. Sometimes a node is called an "eye"; if you think about an eye on a potato, you will have a picture of plant energy waiting to burst forth, and that's how a node is, even though they don't look like a potato eye. Some nodes are quite obvious, and may appear as a thick bulge or a horizontal band on the stem; others are less visible.

Offset. A baby plant that develops off the side of a mature plant, usually tight up against the mother. Eventually, the mother plant will die off, although it may take years.

Rhizome. It looks like a root, but actually it's a specialized kind of stem that grows horizontally on top of the soil or just underneath the surface. New growth originates from it.

Rootbound. A plant is said to be rootbound when its roots have grown so densely that they fill up the space and are growing in circles around the walls of the pot. "Potbound" means the same thing.

Rosette. This word describes a certain pattern of growth. Leaves grow out from a very short central stem all in a circle; if you look down on the plant from above, the leaves are like the petals of a fat rose.

Species. The lowest category in the system of plant classification. The species name is always used in conjunction with the genus name; for example, in *Crassula argentea* (jade plant) *Crassula* is the genus name and *argentea* is the species. We would never say just *argentea,* because by itself it has no meaning.

Spores. The "seeds" of ferns. An individual spore is microscopic; what we see with the naked eye is actually a spore case, a cluster of many spores. It looks like a small brown or black dot on the back side of fern fronds.

Succulent. This word is used in two different but related ways in the world of plants. As a noun, "succulent" is an all-inclusive name for plants that have evolved thick stems or leaves as a way to conserve moisture in their native dry conditions. Many, many species are succulents; there is not a genus called "succulent."

"Succulent" is also used as an adjective; this usage is less precise. We say that stems of a certain plant are succulent when we mean that they are juicy; the plant may or may not be a true succulent.

Transpire. A plant's equivalent of breathing. As part of the total cycle of life, plants give off water vapor and oxygen through their leaves; that process is called transpiration.

Variegated. Leaves that are a mix of colors, rather than all green. Common colors on variegated leaves are white, cream, or yellow; less common are shades of purple, pink, or brown.

Variety. A subspecies that has evolved in nature. Technically different from a cultivar, although the difference is not universally maintained.